Dec 8

# CAMBRIDGE

D0923961

# IELTS

## GENERAL TRAINING 14

WITH ANSWERS

AUTHENTIC PRACTICE TESTS

**Cambridge University Press**
www.cambridge.org/elt

**Cambridge Assessment English**
www.cambridgeenglish.org

Information on this title: www.cambridge.org/9781108717793

First published 2019

20  19  18  17  16  15  14  13  12  11  10  9  8  7  6  5  4  3  2  1

Printed in Malaysia by Vivar Printing

*A catalogue record for this publication is available from the British Library*

ISBN 978-1-108-71779-3 General Training Student's Book with answers
ISBN 978-1-108-68136-0 General Training Student's Book with answers with Audio
ISBN 978-1-108-71777-9 Academic Student's Book with answers
ISBN 978-1-108-68131-5 Academic Student's Book with answers with Audio
ISBN 978-1-108-71860-8 Audio CDs (2)

The publishers have no responsibility for the persistence or accuracy of URLs
for external or third-party internet websites referred to in this publication, and
do not guarantee that any content on such websites is, or will remain, accurate
or appropriate. Information regarding prices, travel timetables, and other factual
information given in this work is correct at the time of first printing but the
publishers do not guarantee the accuracy of such information thereafter.

# Contents

Introduction                                        4

Test 1                                             10

Test 2                                             33

Test 3                                             54

Test 4                                             77

Audioscripts                                       99

Listening and Reading answer keys                 121

Sample answers for Writing tasks                  129

Sample answer sheets                              137

Acknowledgements                                  141

# Introduction

The International English Language Testing System (IELTS) is widely recognised as a reliable means of assessing the language ability of candidates who need to study or work where English is the language of communication. These Practice Tests are designed to give future IELTS candidates an idea of whether their English is at the required level.

IELTS is owned by three partners: Cambridge Assessment English, part of the University of Cambridge; the British Council; IDP Education Pty Limited (through its subsidiary company, IELTS Australia Pty Limited). Further information on IELTS can be found on the IELTS website www.ielts.org.

## WHAT IS THE TEST FORMAT?

IELTS consists of four components. All candidates take the same Listening and Speaking tests. There is a choice of Reading and Writing tests according to whether a candidate is taking the Academic or General Training module.

| Academic | General Training |
|---|---|
| For candidates wishing to study at undergraduate or postgraduate levels, and for those seeking professional registration. | For candidates wishing to migrate to an English-speaking country (Australia, Canada, New Zealand, UK), and for those wishing to train or study at below degree level. |

The test components are taken in the following order:

| Listening | | |
|---|---|---|
| 4 sections, 40 items, approximately 30 minutes | | |
| **Academic Reading** 3 sections, 40 items 60 minutes | or | **General Training Reading** 3 sections, 40 items 60 minutes |
| **Academic Writing** 2 tasks 60 minutes | or | **General Training Writing** 2 tasks 60 minutes |
| **Speaking** 11 to 14 minutes | | |
| **Total Test Time** 2 hours 44 minutes | | |

# GENERAL TRAINING TEST FORMAT

## Listening

This test consists of four sections, each with ten questions. The first two sections are concerned with social needs. The first section is a conversation between two speakers and the second section is a monologue. The final two sections are concerned with situations related to educational or training contexts. The third section is a conversation between up to four people and the fourth section is a monologue.

A variety of question types is used, including: multiple choice, matching, plan/map/diagram labelling, form completion, note completion, table completion, flow-chart completion, summary completion, sentence completion and short-answer questions.

Candidates hear the recording once only and answer the questions as they listen. Ten minutes are allowed at the end for candidates to transfer their answers to the answer sheet.

## Reading

This test consists of three sections with 40 questions. The texts are taken from notices, advertisements, leaflets, newspapers, instruction manuals, books and magazines. The first section contains texts relevant to basic linguistic survival in English, with tasks mainly concerned with providing factual information. The second section focuses on the work context and involves texts of more complex language. The third section involves reading more extended texts, with a more complex structure, but with the emphasis on descriptive and instructive rather than argumentative texts.

A variety of question types is used, including: multiple choice, identifying information (True/False/Not Given), identifying the writer's views/claims (Yes/No/Not Given), matching information, matching headings, matching features, matching sentence endings, sentence completion, summary completion, note completion, table completion, flow-chart completion, diagram label completion and short-answer questions.

## Writing

This test consists of two tasks. It is suggested that candidates spend about 20 minutes on Task 1, which requires them to write at least 150 words, and 40 minutes on Task 2, which requires them to write at least 250 words. Task 2 contributes twice as much as Task 1 to the Writing score.

In Task 1, candidates are asked to respond to a given situation with a letter requesting information or explaining the situation. They are assessed on their ability to engage in personal correspondence, elicit and provide general factual information, express needs, wants, likes and dislikes, express opinions, complaints, etc.

In Task 2, candidates are presented with a point of view, argument or problem. They are assessed on their ability to provide general factual information, outline a problem and present a solution, present and justify an opinion, and to evaluate and challenge ideas, evidence or arguments.

Candidates are also assessed on their ability to write in an appropriate style. More information on assessing the Writing test, including Writing assessment criteria (public version), is available on the IELTS website.

## Speaking

This test takes between 11 and 14 minutes and is conducted by a trained examiner. There are three parts:

*Part 1*

The candidate and the examiner introduce themselves. Candidates then answer general questions about themselves, their home/family, their job/studies, their interests and a wide range of similar familiar topic areas. This part lasts between four and five minutes.

*Part 2*

The candidate is given a task card with prompts and is asked to talk on a particular topic. The candidate has one minute to prepare and they can make some notes if they wish, before speaking for between one and two minutes. The examiner then asks one or two questions on the same topic.

*Part 3*

The examiner and the candidate engage in a discussion of more abstract issues which are thematically linked to the topic in Part 2. The discussion lasts between four and five minutes.

The Speaking test assesses whether candidates can communicate effectively in English. The assessment takes into account Fluency and Coherence, Lexical Resource, Grammatical Range and Accuracy, and Pronunciation. More information on assessing the Speaking test, including Speaking assessment criteria (public version), is available on the IELTS website.

# HOW IS IELTS SCORED?

IELTS results are reported on a nine-band scale. In addition to the score for overall language ability, IELTS provides a score in the form of a profile for each of the four skills (Listening, Reading, Writing and Speaking). These scores are also reported on a nine-band scale. All scores are recorded on the Test Report Form along with details of the candidate's nationality, first language and date of birth. Each Overall Band Score corresponds to a descriptive statement which gives a summary of the English language ability of a candidate classified at that level. The nine bands and their descriptive statements are as follows:

**9 Expert User** – *Has fully operational command of the language: appropriate, accurate and fluent with complete understanding.*

**8 Very Good User** – *Has fully operational command of the language with only occasional unsystematic inaccuracies and inappropriacies. Misunderstandings may occur in unfamiliar situations. Handles complex detailed argumentation well.*

**7 Good User** – *Has operational command of the language, though with occasional inaccuracies, inappropriacies and misunderstandings in some situations. Generally handles complex language well and understands detailed reasoning.*

**6 Competent User** – *Has generally effective command of the language despite some inaccuracies, inappropriacies and misunderstandings. Can use and understand fairly complex language, particularly in familiar situations.*

**5 Modest User** – *Has partial command of the language, coping with overall meaning in most situations, though is likely to make many mistakes. Should be able to handle basic communication in own field.*

**4 Limited User** – *Basic competence is limited to familiar situations. Has frequent problems in understanding and expression. Is not able to use complex language.*

**3 Extremely Limited User** – *Conveys and understands only general meaning in very familiar situations. Frequent breakdowns in communication occur.*

**2 Intermittent User** – *No real communication is possible except for the most basic information using isolated words or short formulae in familiar situations and to meet immediate needs. Has great difficulty understanding spoken and written English.*

**1 Non User** – *Essentially has no ability to use the language beyond possibly a few isolated words.*

**0 Did not attempt the test** – *No assessable information provided.*

# MARKING THE PRACTICE TESTS

## Listening and Reading

The answer keys are on pages 121–128.
Each question in the Listening and Reading tests is worth one mark.

*Questions which require letter / Roman numeral answers*

- For questions where the answers are letters or Roman numerals, you should write *only* the number of answers required. For example, if the answer is a single letter or numeral you should write only one answer. If you have written more letters or numerals than are required, the answer must be marked wrong.

*Questions which require answers in the form of words or numbers*

- Answers may be written in upper or lower case.
- Words in brackets are *optional* – they are correct, but not necessary.
- Alternative answers are separated by a slash (/).
- If you are asked to write an answer using a certain number of words and/or (a) number(s), you will be penalised if you exceed this. For example, if a question specifies an answer using NO MORE THAN THREE WORDS and the correct answer is 'black leather coat', the answer 'coat of black leather' is *incorrect*.
- In questions where you are expected to complete a gap, you should only transfer the necessary missing word(s) onto the answer sheet. For example, to complete 'in the …', where the correct answer is 'morning', the answer 'in the morning' would be *incorrect*.
- All answers require correct spelling (including words in brackets).
- Both US and UK spelling are acceptable and are included in the answer key.
- All standard alternatives for numbers, dates and currencies are acceptable.
- All standard abbreviations are acceptable.
- You will find additional notes about individual answers in the answer key.

## Writing

The sample answers are on pages 129–136. It is not possible for you to give yourself a mark for the Writing tasks. We have provided sample answers (written by candidates), showing their score and the examiner's comments. These sample answers will give you an insight into what is required for the Writing test.

# HOW SHOULD YOU INTERPRET YOUR SCORES?

At the end of each Listening and Reading answer key you will find a chart which will help you assess whether, on the basis of your Practice Test results, you are ready to take the IELTS test.

In interpreting your score, there are a number of points you should bear in mind. Your performance in the real IELTS test will be reported in two ways: there will be a Band Score from 1 to 9 for each of the components and an Overall Band Score from 1 to 9, which is the average of your scores in the four components. However, institutions considering your application are advised to look at both the Overall Band Score and the Bands for each component in order to determine whether you have the language skills needed for a particular course of study or work environment. For example, if you are applying for a course which involves a lot of reading and writing, but no lectures, listening skills might be less important and a score of 5 in Listening might be acceptable if the Overall Band Score was 7. However, for a course which has lots of lectures and spoken instructions, a score of 5 in Listening might be unacceptable even though the Overall Band Score was 7.

Once you have marked your tests, you should have some idea of whether your listening and reading skills are good enough for you to try the IELTS test. If you did well enough in one component, but not in others, you will have to decide for yourself whether you are ready to take the test.

The Practice Tests have been checked to ensure that they are of approximately the same level of difficulty as the real IELTS test. However, we cannot guarantee that your score in the Practice Tests will be reflected in the real IELTS test. The Practice Tests can only give you an idea of your possible future performance and it is ultimately up to you to make decisions based on your score.

Different institutions accept different IELTS scores for different types of courses. We have based our recommendations on the average scores which the majority of institutions accept. The institution to which you are applying may, of course, require a higher or lower score than most other institutions.

## Further information

For more information about IELTS or any other Cambridge Assessment English examination, write to:

Cambridge Assessment English
The Triangle Building
Shaftesbury Road
Cambridge
CB2 8EA
United Kingdom

https://support.cambridgeenglish.org
http://www.ielts.org

# Test 1

**SECTION 1**     *Questions 1–10*

*Complete the form below.*

*Write **ONE WORD AND/OR A NUMBER** for each answer.*

| CRIME REPORT FORM | |
|---|---|
| **Type of crime**: <br> **Personal information** | theft |
| *Example* <br> Name | Louise ........*Taylor*........ |
| Nationality <br> Date of birth <br> Occupation <br> Reason for visit <br> Length of stay <br> Current address | **1** ................................. <br> 14 December 1977 <br> interior designer <br> business (to buy antique **2** .............................) <br> two months <br> **3** ................................ Apartments (No 15) |
| **Details of theft** <br> Items stolen <br><br> Date of theft | <br> – a wallet containing approximately **4** £ ...................... <br> – a **5** ................................ <br> **6** ................................ |
| **Possible time and place of theft** <br> Location <br> Details of suspect | <br> outside the **7** ........................ at about 4 pm <br> – some boys asked for the **8** ........................ then ran off <br> – one had a T-shirt with a picture of a tiger <br> – he was about 12, slim build with **9** ........................ hair |
| **Crime reference number allocated** <br>      **10** ................................ | |

## SECTION 2    *Questions 11–20*

# Induction talk for new apprentices

*Questions 11 and 12*

*Choose **TWO** letters, **A–E**.*

Which **TWO** pieces of advice for the first week of an apprenticeship does the manager give?

    **A**    get to know colleagues
    **B**    learn from any mistakes
    **C**    ask lots of questions
    **D**    react positively to feedback
    **E**    enjoy new challenges

*Questions 13 and 14*

*Choose **TWO** letters, **A–E**.*

Which **TWO** things does the manager say mentors can help with?

    **A**    confidence-building
    **B**    making career plans
    **C**    completing difficult tasks
    **D**    making a weekly timetable
    **E**    reviewing progress

*Questions 15–20*

What does the manager say about each of the following aspects of the company policy for apprentices?

*Write the correct letter, **A**, **B** or **C**, next to Questions 15–20.*

| | |
|---|---|
| **A** | It is encouraged. |
| **B** | There are some restrictions. |
| **C** | It is against the rules. |

**Company policy for apprentices**

15  Using the internet         .....................

16  Flexible working           .....................

17  Booking holidays           .....................

18  Working overtime           .....................

19  Wearing trainers           .....................

20  Bringing food to work      .....................

# SECTION 3    *Questions 21–30*

*Questions 21–25*

*Choose the correct letter, **A**, **B** or **C**.*

## Cities built by the sea

21  Carla and Rob were surprised to learn that coastal cities

  A    contain nearly half the world's population.
  B    include most of the world's largest cities.
  C    are growing twice as fast as other cities.

22  According to Rob, building coastal cities near to rivers

  A    may bring pollution to the cities.
  B    may reduce the land available for agriculture.
  C    may mean the countryside is spoiled by industry.

23  What mistake was made when building water drainage channels in Miami in the 1950s?

  A    There were not enough of them.
  B    They were made of unsuitable materials.
  C    They did not allow for the effects of climate change.

24  What do Rob and Carla think that the authorities in Miami should do immediately?

  A    take measures to restore ecosystems
  B    pay for a new flood prevention system
  C    stop disposing of waste materials into the ocean

25  What do they agree should be the priority for international action?

  A    greater coordination of activities
  B    more sharing of information
  C    agreement on shared policies

*Questions 26–30*

What decision do the students make about each of the following parts of their presentation?

*Choose **FIVE** answers from the box and write the correct letter, **A–G**, next to Questions 26–30.*

| Decisions |
| --- |
| **A** use visuals |
| **B** keep it short |
| **C** involve other students |
| **D** check the information is accurate |
| **E** provide a handout |
| **F** focus on one example |
| **G** do online research |

**Parts of the presentation**

26  Historical background      ....................

27  Geographical factors       ....................

28  Past mistakes              ....................

29  Future risks               ....................

30  International implications  ....................

## SECTION 4    *Questions 31–40*

*Complete the notes below.*

*Write ONE WORD ONLY for each answer.*

---

### Marine renewable energy (ocean energy)

**Introduction**

More energy required because of growth in population and **31** ...................................

What's needed:

• renewable energy sources

• methods that won't create pollution

**Wave energy**

Advantage: waves provide a **32** ................................... source of renewable energy

Electricity can be generated using offshore or onshore systems

Onshore systems may use a reservoir

Problems:

• waves can move in any **33** ...................................

• movement of sand, etc. on the **34** ................................... of the ocean may be affected

**Tidal energy**

Tides are more **35** ................................... than waves

Planned tidal lagoon in Wales:

• will be created in a **36** ................................... at Swansea

• breakwater (dam) containing 16 turbines

• rising tide forces water through turbines, generating electricity

• stored water is released through **37** ................................... , driving the turbines in the reverse direction

Advantages:

• not dependent on weather

• no **38** ................................... is required to make it work

• likely to create a number of **39** ...................................

Problem:

• may harm fish and birds, e.g. by affecting **40** ................................... and building up silt

**Ocean thermal energy conversion**

Uses a difference in temperature between the surface and lower levels
Water brought to the surface in a pipe

---

**READING**

## SECTION 1   *Questions 1–14*

*Read the text below and answer Questions 1–6.*

# TRANSITION CARE FOR THE ELDERLY

### What is transition care?

Transition care is for older people who have been receiving medical treatment, but need more help to recover, and time to make a decision about the best place for them to live in the longer term. You can only access transition care directly from hospital.

Transition care is focused on individual goals and therapies and is given for a limited time only. It offers access to a package of services that may include:

- low-intensity therapy such as physiotherapy (exercise, mobility, strength and balance) and podiatry (foot care)
- access to a social worker
- nursing support for clinical care such as wound care
- personal care.

### Who provides transition care services?

Transition care is often provided by non-government organisations and is subsidised by the government. If your circumstances allow, it is expected you'll contribute to the cost of your care.

Daily care fees are set by the organisation that provides your transition care services (your service provider). They should explain these fees to you, and the amount charged should form part of the agreement between you and the service provider. The fee is calculated on a daily basis.

### Where do I receive transition care?

Transition care is provided in your own home or in a 'live-in' setting. This setting can be part of an existing aged-care home or health facility such as a separate wing of a hospital.

### What if I'm already receiving services through a different programme?

If you're already receiving subsidised residential care in an aged-care home, but you need to go somewhere else for transition care, your place in the aged-care home will be held until you return.

*Questions 1–6*

Do the following statements agree with the information given in the text on page 16?

*In boxes 1–6 on your answer sheet, write*

> **TRUE**　　　　*if the statement agrees with the information*
> **FALSE**　　　　*if the statement contradicts the information*
> **NOT GIVEN**　*if there is no information on this*

1　Only hospital patients can go on to have transition care.

2　Transition care may be long term or short term.

3　Everyone receiving transition care must contribute to the cost.

4　Transition care at home is only available for patients who live alone.

5　Transition care may be given on a hospital site.

6　You may lose your place in a care home if you have to leave it to receive transition care.

*Read the text below and answer Questions 7–14.*

# CABIN BAGS FOR AIR TRAVEL

*If you want a small bag with wheels that you can take onto the plane with you, there's a wide choice. Here are some of the best.*

A   The **Flyer B3** is an ultra-lightweight cabin bag which can withstand some pretty harsh treatment. Its nylon and polyester sides won't rip or burst open if it's dropped or thrown whilst in transit. However, the trolley handle feels quite thin and flimsy. The top carrying handle is hard and flat, and the side handle isn't easy to grip.

B   The **Lightglide** has two external pockets, both of which are zipped and lockable, but the inside pocket does not zip. In tests, we found the contents remain dry when given a good soaking, even around the zips. The trolley handle has a choice of two heights and the plastic hand grip doesn't have any sharp ridges that'll make your hands sore. For carrying there are fabric handles at the top and side.

C   The **Foxton** is easy to control across most surfaces. However, the zips don't always run smoothly especially around the corners, so you may have to give them a good tug, especially if the case is very full. This is definitely one to avoid if you're going somewhere rainy as it lets loads of water in, and documents in the pockets will also get pretty wet unless they're in plastic folders.

D   The **Skybag** has a single external zipped pocket and another located inside the lid. Your clothes are kept in place by two adjustable straps. The zips are easy to grip and they run smoothly around the case. However, this cabin bag felt a little heavy to pull on all but smooth floors, and it was hard to steer compared with some of the other suitcases.

E   The **Travelsure 35** is available in a huge range of fabric designs including leopard print or lipstick kisses. The retractable trolley handle is comfortable but can't be adjusted to suit users of different heights. There's no internal divider, but there are two handy zipped pockets in the lid. We test each bag by letting it fall onto a hard floor – and our results show that you'll have to treat this bag with great care if you want it to last. The fabric tore so badly at one of the corners that it was unusable.

*Questions 7–14*

The text on page 18 has five paragraphs, **A–E**.

Which paragraph mentions the following?

*Write the correct letter, **A–E**, in boxes 7–14 on your answer sheet.*

**NB** *You may use any letter more than once.*

7    The zips on this cabin bag may be difficult to use.

8    This cabin bag may be badly damaged if it is dropped.

9    The handles of this cabin bag have a number of different problems.

10   This cabin bag is very resistant to water.

11   There's a good choice of patterns for the fabric of this cabin bag.

12   This cabin bag isn't very easy to move around.

13   This cabin bag has just one internal zipped pocket.

14   The trolley handle of this cabin bag is adjustable.

## SECTION 2    *Questions 15–27*

*Read the text below and answer Questions 15–20.*

# College car parking policy – staff

### Parking permits and tickets
Staff permits are required to park a motor vehicle (other than a motorcycle parked in the cycle bays) on campus between 8.30 am and 4.30 pm, Monday to Friday, during term time. Annual permits can be purchased from the Hospitality Department. Application forms can be downloaded from the College website. All permits/tickets must be clearly displayed in the windscreen of vehicles during the dates of term time, as published in the academic calendar. Please inform the Services Administrator of any changes to registration details on telephone ext. 406. Annual car parking permits can be purchased from 20th September and are valid for one academic year from 1st October to 30th June. The annual charges for car parking are displayed on the application form.

### Enforcement
The nominated contractor will issue fixed Penalty Charge Notices (see below) on vehicles that fail to display a valid permit and/or parking ticket, or vehicles that are parked on yellow lines or in disabled parking bays without displaying a blue disabled-parking permit. Reductions of parking space availability may arise in order to accommodate College recruitment activities and/or estate development/maintenance projects. Vehicles that are in breach of the policy will be issued with a Penalty Charge Notice.

### Penalty Charge Notice (PCN)
The PCN is £30, increasing to £60 seven days after issue. The nominated contractor is responsible for the collection of unpaid PCNs and may use legal action where necessary to recover unpaid PCNs. If issued with a PCN, appeals must be taken up directly with the parking enforcement company (details included on the notice) **not** the college.

### Disabled parking
The college has designated car parking spaces for disabled car drivers. The college will make all reasonable efforts to ensure these parking spaces are used only by drivers who display their blue disabled-parking permits, and a valid pay-and-display or annual permit, as appropriate.

If issues arise concerning the availability of the parking spaces, those concerned should raise the matter with the Domestic Services Department in order to effect a temporary solution.

## Visitors

The College welcomes visitors and provides parking arrangements through pre-arranged permits, which must be displayed in the vehicle. Please contact the Hospitality Department for further information. On Open Days, sections of car parking on campus may be reserved for visitors.

## Short-term drop-off/pick-up provision

There will be two short-term drop-off/pick-up spaces for users of the nursery, with a maximum of ten minutes' waiting time allowed. These are located outside Concorde Building. The nursery staff bays may not be used under any circumstances.

Questions 15–20

Answer the questions below.

Choose **NO MORE THAN THREE WORDS AND/OR A NUMBER** from the text for each answer.

Write your answers in boxes 15–20 on your answer sheet.

15  Where can you buy parking permits at the college?

16  Which document shows the dates of term time?

17  What is the start date of annual parking permits?

18  Who is responsible for giving out parking fines if you park in the wrong place?

19  What do visitors need to show when parking?

20  Where can the nursery pick-up point be found?

*Read the text below and answer Questions 21–27.*

# Maternity benefits

If you are expecting a baby, there are a number of benefit schemes that could help you financially. However, eligibility differs for each individual scheme.

### Statutory Maternity Pay (SMP)

You may be entitled to Statutory Maternity Pay (SMP) from your employer. This is a weekly payment, to help make it easier for you to take time off, both before and after the birth of your baby. SMP can be paid for up to 39 weeks.

You are entitled to SMP if you have been employed by the same company for at least 26 weeks by the end of the 15th week before your baby is due. You must also be earning an average of at least £87 per week (before tax). The amount you get depends on how much you earn. For 6 weeks, you will receive 90% of your average weekly earnings. Then you will receive £112.75 per week for the remaining 33 weeks.

### Maternity Allowance (MA)

Maternity Allowance (MA) is available to those who are employed or self-employed but not eligible for Statutory Maternity Pay (SMP). You may be entitled to Maternity Allowance if you have been employed or self-employed for at least 26 weeks in the 66 weeks before you are due to give birth. You don't have to work for the same employer for those 26 weeks. You also don't have to work full weeks (as a part week counts as a full week) during the same period. Maternity Allowance can be paid for up to 39 weeks, and is either paid at the same standard rate as SMP or 90% of your average weekly earnings. You'll receive whichever amount is the lower. You can find Maternity Allowance forms at antenatal clinics throughout the country.

### Child Tax Credit

If you're on a low income, over 16, and are responsible for at least one child, you may also be entitled to Child Tax Credit. The amount you get will depend on your personal circumstances and income. When your income is being assessed, any child benefit, maintenance payments or Maternity Allowance payments will not be classed as income. This means that it will not be taken into account when calculating your Child Tax Credit.

### Sure Start Maternity Payments

If you get benefits or Child Tax Credit because you're on a low income, then you may be entitled to Sure Start Maternity Payments. These are individual grants to help towards the cost of a new baby.

*Questions 21–27*

*Answer the questions below.*

*Choose **NO MORE THAN TWO WORDS AND/OR A NUMBER** from the text for each answer.*

*Write your answers in boxes 21–27 on your answer sheet.*

21  What is the minimum period you must have worked for an employer in order to be eligible for SMP?

22  For how long is SMP payable every week as a percentage of your average weekly earnings?

23  What sum is payable every week as the second part of SMP entitlement?

24  What is the maximum length of time MA is payable?

25  Where can MA forms be obtained?

26  Apart from income, what else is considered when assessing how much Child Tax Credit is paid?

27  What are Sure Start Maternity Payments?

# SECTION 3    *Questions 28–40*

*Questions 28–32*

The text on pages 26 and 27 has five sections, **A–E**.

*Choose the correct heading for each section from the list of headings below.*

*Write the correct number, **i–viii**, in boxes 28–32 on your answer sheet.*

| List of Headings |
| --- |
| **i** Solving the puzzle of a papyrus document |
| **ii** The importance of written records and different ways of recording them |
| **iii** The use of papyrus for a range of purposes |
| **iv** Suggestions for future possibilities for papyrus |
| **v** How papyrus was cultivated and different manufacturing methods |
| **vi** The decline of papyrus use |
| **vii** The preservation and destruction of papyrus documents |
| **viii** The process of papyrus production |

**28**  Section A

**29**  Section B

**30**  Section C

**31**  Section D

**32**  Section E

# PAPYRUS

*Used by the ancient Egyptians to make paper, the papyrus plant has helped to shape the world we live in*

**A**     Libraries and archives are cultural crossroads of knowledge exchange, where the past transmits information to the present, and where the present has the opportunity to inform the future. Bureaucracies have become the backbone of civilizations, as governments try to keep track of populations, business transactions and taxes. At a personal level, our lives are governed by the documents we possess; we are certified on paper literally from birth to death. And written documentation carries enormous cultural importance: consider the consequences of signing the Foundation Document of the United Nations or the Convention on Biological Diversity.

Documentation requires a writing tool and a surface upon which to record the information permanently. About 5,000 years ago, the Sumerians started to use reeds or sticks to make marks on mud blocks which were then baked, but, despite being fireproof, these were difficult to store. Other cultures used more flexible but less permanent surfaces, including animal skins and wood strips. In western culture, the adoption of papyrus was to have a great impact. Sheets of papyrus not only provide an invaluable record of people's daily lives, they can also be dated using carbon-dating techniques, giving precise information about the age of the text written on them.

**B**     Papyrus is strongly associated with Egyptian culture, although all the ancient civilizations around the Mediterranean used it. The papyrus sedge is a tall grass-like plant. It was harvested from shallow water and swamplands on the banks of the River Nile. Manufacturing sheets of papyrus from papyrus sedge was a complex, messy process. Pith from inside the plant's stem was cut into long strips that were laid side by side. These were then covered with a second layer of strips which were laid at right angles to the first, then soaked in water and hammered together. The sheet was then crushed to extract the water, dried and then polished to produce a high-quality writing surface. Individual sheets could be glued together and rolled up to make scrolls or folded and bound to form books.

**C**     In moist climates the cellulose-rich sheets of papyrus would readily decay, becoming covered by mould or full of holes from attacks by insects. But in dry climates, such as the Middle East, papyrus is a stable, rot-resistant writing surface. The earliest known roll of papyrus scroll was found in the tomb of an official called Hemeka near Memphis, which was then the capital city of Egypt, and is around five thousand years old. In 79CE, nearly 2,000 papyrus scrolls in the library of Julius Caesar's father-in-law were protected at Herculaneum by ash from the catastrophic

From Stephen Harris, *What have Plants Ever Done for Us?*, Bodleian Library Publishing 2015. Reprinted by kind permission of Bodleian Library Publishing.

eruption of Mount Vesuvius. However, the most famous discoveries of papyrus have come from the rubbish dumps of the ancient town of Oxyrhynchus, some 160km south-west of Cairo, in the desert to the west of the Nile. Oxyrhynchus was a regional administrative capital and for a thousand years generated vast amounts of administrative documentation, including accounts, tax returns and correspondence, which was periodically discarded to make room for more. Over time, a thick layer of sand covered these dumps, and they were forgotten. But the documents were protected by the sand, creating a time capsule that allowed astonishing glimpses into the lives of the town's inhabitants over hundreds of years.

Collections of documents that record information and ideas have frequently been viewed as potentially dangerous. For thousands of years, governments, despots and conquerors have resorted to burning libraries and books to rid themselves of inconvenient evidence or obliterate cultures and ideas that they found politically, morally or religiously unacceptable. One such calamity, the burning of the Great Library of Alexandria, and the papyrus scrolls and books it contained, has been mythologized and has come to symbolize the global loss of cultural knowledge.

**D**  Besides their use in record-keeping, papyrus stems were used in many other aspects of Mediterranean life, such as for boat construction and making ropes, sails and baskets, as well as being a source of food. In 1969 the adventurer Thor Heyerdahl attempted to cross the Atlantic from Morocco in the boat *Ra*, to show that it was possible for mariners in ancient times to cross the Atlantic Ocean. *Ra* was made from bundles of papyrus stems and modelled on ancient Egyptian craft. As a marshland plant, papyrus sedge stabilizes soils and reduces erosion, while some investigations show that it has potential for water purification and sewage treatment.

**E**  True paper was probably invented in China in the first century CE. Like papyrus, it was constructed from a meshwork of plant fibres, but the Chinese used fibres from the white mulberry tree, which yielded a tough, flexible material that could be folded, stretched, and compressed. The adoption of this paper by western cultures soon rendered papyrus obsolete.

Despite dreams of paper-free societies, western cultures still use enormous quantities of paper, often in ways that it would be inconceivable to use papyrus for. As a paper substitute, the role of the papyrus sedge in western cultures has been superseded; papyrus is little more than a niche product for the tourist market. What makes papyrus noteworthy for western societies nowadays is its use as the surface upon which our ancient ancestors recorded their lives, their art and their science. In the words of the ancient Roman philosopher Pliny the Elder, it is 'the material on which the immortality of human beings depends'.

---

From Stephen Harris, *What have Plants Ever Done for Us?*, Bodleian Library Publishing 2015. Reprinted by kind permission of Bodleian Library Publishing.

*Questions 33–37*

*Choose the correct letter, **A, B, C** or **D**.*

*Write the correct letter in boxes 33–37 on your answer sheet.*

**33** What was the problem with using animal skins and wood strips for writing on?

    **A** They did not last for a long time.
    **B** They were not easy to store.
    **C** They were insufficiently flexible.
    **D** They could be destroyed by fire.

**34** Why did papyrus manufacturers hammer the papyrus?

    **A** to remove water from the pith strips
    **B** to join the layers of pith strips together
    **C** to allow the pith strips to be easily cut
    **D** to position the layers of pith strips at the correct angle

**35** When referring to burning libraries and books, the writer is suggesting that

    **A** information can be used for harm as well as for good.
    **B** new ways must be found to ensure information is not lost.
    **C** cultural knowledge depends on more than written texts.
    **D** those in power may wish to keep others in ignorance.

**36** The writer refers to Thor Heyerdahl to illustrate the point that

    **A** papyrus could be used as a food on long sea voyages.
    **B** the ancient Egyptians already had advanced navigation skills.
    **C** papyrus could be used to build boats for long sea journeys.
    **D** the ancient Egyptians knew of the environmental benefits of papyrus.

**37** What does the writer conclude about papyrus today?

    **A** It is better for the environment than using paper.
    **B** Its significance is restricted to its role in the past.
    **C** It is still the best writing surface for some purposes.
    **D** More efforts need to be made to ensure it stays in use.

*Questions 38–40*

*Complete the summary below.*

*Choose **ONE WORD ONLY** from the text for each answer.*

*Write your answers in boxes 38–40 on your answer sheet.*

## How papyrus documents have survived

Papyrus is rich in cellulose and in some conditions will be destroyed by fungal growths or be consumed by **38** ................................................. . However, it can survive for long periods in an environment that is dry. It has been found in a 5,000-year-old **39** ...................................... in Egypt, and in Herculaneum many papyrus documents were preserved following a huge **40** ................................. in 79 CE. In the town of Oxyrhynchus, unwanted administrative documents were left on rubbish dumps which were covered with sand, preserving them for many years.

## WRITING

# WRITING TASK 1

You should spend about 20 minutes on this task.

---

*You have seen an advertisement in an Australian magazine for someone to live with a family for six months and look after their six-year-old child.*

*Write a letter to the parents. In your letter*

- *explain why you would like the job*
- *give details of why you would be a suitable person to employ*
- *say how you would spend your free time while you are in Australia*

---

Write at least 150 words.

You do **NOT** need to write any addresses.

Begin your letter as follows:

**Dear Sir or Madam,**

# WRITING TASK 2

You should spend about 40 minutes on this task.

Write about the following topic:

---

*The growth of online shopping will one day lead to all shops in towns and cities closing.*

*Do you agree or disagree?*

---

Give reasons for your answer and include any relevant examples from your own knowledge or experience.

Write at least 250 words.

# SPEAKING

## PART 1

The examiner asks the candidate about him/herself, his/her home, work or studies and other familiar topics.

**EXAMPLE**

**Future**

- What job would you like to have ten years from now? [Why?]
- How useful will English be for your future? [Why/Why not?]
- How much travelling do you hope to do in the future? [Why/Why not?]
- How do you think your life will change in the future? [Why/Why not?]

## PART 2

> **Describe a book that you enjoyed reading because you had to think a lot.**
>
> **You should say:**
>     **what this book was**
>     **why you decided to read it**
>     **what reading this book made you think about**
>
> **and explain why you enjoyed reading this book.**

You will have to talk about the topic for one to two minutes. You have one minute to think about what you are going to say. You can make some notes to help you if you wish.

## PART 3

*Discussion topics:*

**Children and reading**

*Example questions:*
What are the most popular types of children's books in your country?
What are the benefits of parents reading books to their children?
Should parents always let children choose the books they read?

**Electronic books**

*Example questions:*
How popular are electronic books are in your country?
What are the advantages of parents reading electronic books (compared to printed books)?
Will electronic books ever completely replace printed books in the future?

# Test 2

## SECTION 1    *Questions 1–10*

*Complete the notes below.*

*Write **ONE WORD AND/OR A NUMBER** for each answer.*

| TOTAL HEALTH CLINIC |
| --- |

**PATIENT DETAILS**

**Personal information**

*Example*

| Name | Julie Anne ......*Garcia*...... |
| --- | --- |

| | |
| --- | --- |
| Contact phone | **1** ................................ |
| Date of birth | **2** ................................ , 1992 |
| Occupation | works as a **3** ................................ |
| Insurance company | **4** ................................ Life Insurance |

**Details of the problem**

| | |
| --- | --- |
| Type of problem | pain in her left **5** ................................ |
| When it began | **6** ................................ ago |
| Action already taken | has taken painkillers and applied ice |

**Other information**

| | |
| --- | --- |
| Sports played | belongs to a **7** ................................ club |
| | goes **8** ................................ regularly |
| Medical history | injured her **9** ................................ last year |
| | no allergies |
| | no regular medication apart from **10** ................................ |

## SECTION 2    *Questions 11–20*

*Questions 11–15*

*Choose the correct letter, **A**, **B** or **C**.*

# Visit to Branley Castle

11    Before Queen Elizabeth I visited the castle in 1576,

   **A**    repairs were carried out to the guest rooms.
   **B**    a new building was constructed for her.
   **C**    a fire damaged part of the main hall.

12    In 1982, the castle was sold to

   **A**    the government.
   **B**    the Fenys family.
   **C**    an entertainment company.

13    In some of the rooms, visitors can

   **A**    speak to experts on the history of the castle.
   **B**    interact with actors dressed as famous characters.
   **C**    see models of historical figures moving and talking.

14    In the castle park, visitors can

   **A**    see an 800-year-old tree.
   **B**    go to an art exhibition.
   **C**    visit a small zoo.

15    At the end of the visit, the group will have

   **A**    afternoon tea in the conservatory.
   **B**    the chance to meet the castle's owners.
   **C**    a photograph together on the Great Staircase.

*Questions 16–20*

*Label the plan below.*

*Write the correct letter, **A–H**, next to Questions 16–20.*

**Branley Castle**

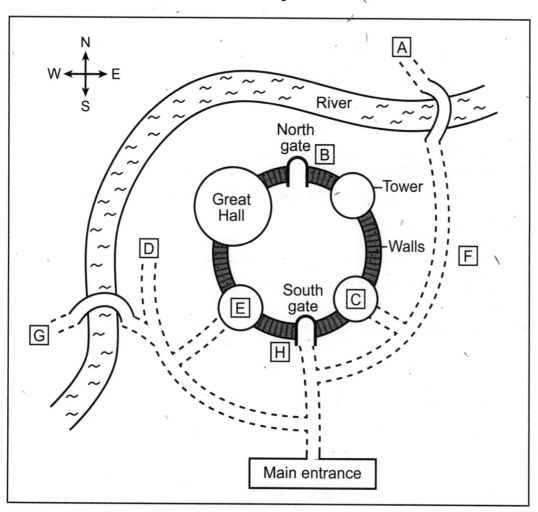

16  Starting point for walking the walls ..................

17  Bow and arrow display ..................

18  Hunting birds display ..................

19  Traditional dancing ..................

20  Shop ..................

## SECTION 3      *Questions 21–30*

Questions 21–24

*Choose the correct letter, **A**, **B** or **C**.*

# Woolly mammoths on St Paul's Island

**21**   How will Rosie and Martin introduce their presentation?

   **A**   with a drawing of woolly mammoths in their natural habitat
   **B**   with a timeline showing when woolly mammoths lived
   **C**   with a video clip about woolly mammoths

**22**   What was surprising about the mammoth tooth found by Russell Graham?

   **A**   It was still embedded in the mammoth's jawbone.
   **B**   It was from an unknown species of mammoth.
   **C**   It was not as old as mammoth remains from elsewhere.

**23**   The students will use an animated diagram to demonstrate how the mammoths

   **A**   became isolated on the island.
   **B**   spread from the island to other areas.
   **C**   coexisted with other animals on the island.

**24**   According to Martin, what is unusual about the date of the mammoths' extinction on the island?

   **A**   how exact it is
   **B**   how early it is
   **C**   how it was established

*Questions 25–30*

What action will the students take for each of the following sections of their presentation?

*Choose **SIX** answers from the box and write the correct letter, **A–H**, next to Questions 25–30.*

| Actions |
| --- |
| **A**  make it more interactive |
| **B**  reduce visual input |
| **C**  add personal opinions |
| **D**  contact one of the researchers |
| **E**  make detailed notes |
| **F**  find information online |
| **G**  check timing |
| **H**  organise the content more clearly |

**Sections of presentation**

**25**  Introduction                                              ......................

**26**  Discovery of the mammoth tooth          ......................

**27**  Initial questions asked by the researchers   ......................

**28**  Further research carried out on the island   ......................

**29**  Findings and possible explanations         ......................

**30**  Relevance to the present day                ......................

## SECTION 4    *Questions 31–40*

*Complete the notes below.*

*Write **ONE WORD ONLY** for each answer.*

# The history of weather forecasting

**Ancient cultures**

* many cultures believed that floods and other disasters were involved in the creation of the world

* many cultures invented **31** ........................... and other ceremonies to make the weather gods friendly

* people needed to observe and interpret the sky to ensure their **32** ...........................

* around 650 BC, Babylonians started forecasting, using weather phenomena such as **33** ...........................

* by 300 BC, the Chinese had a calendar made up of a number of **34** ........................... connected with the weather

**Ancient Greeks**

* a more scientific approach

* Aristotle tried to explain the formation of various weather phenomena

* Aristotle also described haloes and **35** ...........................

**Middle Ages**

* Aristotle's work considered accurate

* many proverbs, e.g. about the significance of the colour of the **36** ..........................., passed on accurate information.

**15th–19th centuries**

* 15th century: scientists recognised value of **37** ........................... for the first time

* Galileo invented the **38** ...........................

* Pascal showed relationship between atmospheric pressure and altitude

* from the 17th century, scientists could measure atmospheric pressure and temperature

* 18th century: Franklin identified the movement of **39** ...........................

* 19th century: data from different locations could be sent to the same place by **40** ...........................

## READING

### SECTION 1    *Questions 1–14*

*Read the text below and answer Questions 1–7.*

# Five reviews of the Wellington Hotel

**A**    My husband and I first stayed at the Wellington a few years ago, and we've returned every year since then. When we arrive and check in, we're always treated like old friends by the staff, so we very much feel at home. Our one disappointment during our last visit was that our room overlooked the car park, but that didn't spoil our stay.

**B**    The hotel hardly seems to have changed in the last hundred years, and we prefer that to many modern hotels, which tend to look the same as each other. The Wellington has character! Our room was very comfortable and quite spacious. We can strongly recommend the breakfast, though we had to wait for a table as the hotel was so full. That was a bit annoying, and there was also nowhere to sit in the lounge.

**C**    We made our reservation by phone without problem, but when we arrived the receptionist couldn't see it on the computer system. Luckily there was a room available. It wasn't quite what we would have chosen, but it was a pleasure to sit in it with a cup of tea, and look out at the swimmers and surfers in the sea.

**D**    We'd be happy to stay at the Wellington again. Although there's nothing special about the rooms, the view from the lounge is lovely, and the restaurant staff were friendly and efficient. Breakfast was a highlight – there was so much on offer we could hardly decide what to eat. We'd stay another time just for that!

**E**    The staff all did their jobs efficiently, and were very helpful when we asked for information about the area. The only difficulty we had was making our reservation online – it wasn't clear whether payment for our deposit went through or not, and I had to call the hotel to find out. Still, once we'd arrived, everything went very smoothly, and we had a delicious dinner in the restaurant.

*Questions 1–7*

*Look at the five online reviews of the Wellington Hotel, **A–E**, on page 39.*

Which review mentions the following?

*Write the correct letter, **A–E**, in boxes 1–7 on your answer sheet.*

**NB** *You may use any letter more than once.*

1    liking the view from the bedroom window

2    finding the receptionists welcoming

3    being pleased with the bedroom

4    becoming confused when booking a room

5    being impressed by the wide choice of food

6    staying in the hotel regularly

7    finding it inconvenient that the hotel was crowded

*Read the text below and answer Questions 8–14.*

# Come and play walking football or walking netball

Walking football and netball have become increasingly popular in recent years, but do you know you can take part in this area? The names make it clear what they are – two of the country's favourite sports where, instead of running, the players walk. It's as simple as that.

Walking football was invented in the UK in 2011, but it was a 2014 TV commercial for a bank, showing it providing financial support to someone who wanted to set up a website for the game, that brought it to people's attention. Since then, tens of thousands of people – mostly, though not only, over the age of 50 – have started playing, and there are more than 800 walking football clubs. Both men and women play walking football, but at the moment the netball teams consist only of women. However, men are beginning to show an interest in playing.

The two games are designed to help people to be active or get fit, whatever their age and level of fitness. In particular, they were invented to encourage older men and women to get more exercise, and to give them a chance to meet other people. Regular physical activity helps to maintain energy, strength and flexibility. You can start gently and do a little more each session. The benefits include lower heart rate and blood pressure, greater mobility, less fat and more muscle.

Many players have given up a sport – either through age or injury – and can now take it up again. They're great ways for people to enjoy a sport they used to play and love, and keep active at the same time, though people who have never played the standard game before are also very welcome.

The local council's Active Lifestyles Team runs sessions at all the council's leisure centres. Come alone or with a friend, and enjoy a friendly game on Monday or Saturday afternoons, or Tuesday or Thursday evenings. Each session costs £3 per person, and you don't have to come regularly or at the same time each week. Our aim is to set up netball and football clubs as soon as there are enough regular players.

*Questions 8–14*

Do the following statements agree with the information given in the text on page 41?

*In boxes 8–14 on your answer sheet, write*

> **TRUE**          *if the statement agrees with the information*
> **FALSE**         *if the statement contradicts the information*
> **NOT GIVEN**  *if there is no information on this*

8    Walking football became well-known when a club featured in a TV programme about the sport.

9    The majority of walking netball players are men.

10   Most clubs arrange social activities for their members.

11   Players are tested regularly to measure changes in their fitness.

12   People who have never played football are encouraged to play walking football.

13   People can take part in the Active Lifestyles Team's sessions whenever they wish.

14   The Active Lifestyles Team intends to start clubs in the future.

## SECTION 2    *Questions 15–27*

*Read the text below and answer Questions 15–20.*

# Dress regulations at work

Your contract may state that you need to dress in a certain manner or wear a uniform. Your contract might also state that you need to dress 'smartly', rather than specifying any particular garments. As you might well have conflicting ideas of what counts as 'smart', you should ask your employer for clarification. Many employers that have a strict dress code choose to provide clothing or a discount on clothing. However, this is not necessarily compulsory for the employer and is a factor you need to consider when taking a job.

### Protective clothing and equipment

Your employer can tell you to put on protective clothing and equipment (such as gloves, a visor, boots, etc.). If you don't, your employer is entitled to take disciplinary action, which can include excluding you from the workplace.

You are required to:
- co-operate with your employer on health and safety
- correctly use work items provided by your employer, including protective equipment, in accordance with instructions
- not interfere with or misuse anything provided for your health and safety or welfare.

Of course, any protective gear has to fit and be appropriate for the situation. It shouldn't cause you pain. If it does, you should negotiate alternative equipment or arrangements. Don't be put off. Sometimes employers can, out of caution, interpret health and safety rules unnecessarily rigidly. And of course you shouldn't be required to pay for any protective equipment or clothing that you need. However, if your employer buys the gear, they are entitled to keep it when you leave.

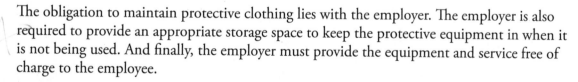

The obligation to maintain protective clothing lies with the employer. The employer is also required to provide an appropriate storage space to keep the protective equipment in when it is not being used. And finally, the employer must provide the equipment and service free of charge to the employee.

### Jewellery

Banning employees from wearing jewellery and loose clothing may be justified to prevent a potential hygiene hazard if you work in areas of food production or areas which need to be kept sterile.

Likewise, your employer can judge that loose jewellery may constitute a snagging hazard if you operate machinery. If you think restrictions are not justified by health and safety concerns, talk to your workplace union rep if you have one, as they may know of solutions to the problem which other employees have used before.

*Questions 15–20*

*Complete the sentences below.*

*Choose **ONE WORD ONLY** from the text for each answer.*

*Write your answers in boxes 15–20 on your answer sheet.*

15  If employees are unsure what their company wishes them to wear for work, they should request ..................................... .

16  Some companies offer their employees a ..................................... when they buy items to wear for work.

17  Employees who fail to wear protective clothing when required could be subject to ..................................... procedures.

18  Employees ought not to be in ..................................... because of protective clothing or equipment.

19  It is the company's responsibility to ensure that there is a suitable place for the ..................................... of protective equipment.

20  Employees who work with certain types of ..................................... may have to remove jewellery to avoid potential injuries.

*Read the text below and answer Questions 21–27.*

# How to achieve a better work–life balance

As more and more employees work from home full time and everyone has 24/7 access to email, balancing work and family may not seem like an easily attainable goal. So how can you juggle the demands of both worlds? Below are some tips to help you get started.

It's easy to get sucked into habits that make us less efficient without realizing it – like keeping your social media page open at work so you don't miss something 'important'. Draw up a list with all the activities that don't enhance your life or career. Then minimize the time you spend on them.

It's hard to say 'no', especially to a supervisor or loved one, but sometimes that powerful little word is essential. Learn to use 'no' judiciously and it will become a powerful tool in balancing work and family.

Research shows that exercise helps you remain alert. Finding time to hit the gym may be hard, but it will ultimately help you get more things done because exercise really boosts energy and improves your ability to concentrate.

Study after study shows that significant sleep deprivation affects your health and well-being. Exposure to electronics can significantly negatively impact your sleep, so try to unplug an hour before you go to sleep.

What would you do if you had a whole day to yourself with no demands on your time? While most people don't have the luxury of a whole day dedicated to relaxation, constantly putting off that downtime and putting everyone's needs before yours will wear you down. Pick a time to do something just for you. Even just a few minutes of 'me time' a day will help to recharge your batteries.

Don't assume your family and manager are aware of your concerns. If you feel you have to adjust your schedule to discover a better work–life balance, then voice that requirement. If that means asking your boss for permission to leave a few minutes early once a week so you can hit that yoga class on the way home, do it.

All new habits require time to build, so if you find yourself sneaking your smartphone to bed, that's okay. Leave your phone downstairs tomorrow night. Tiny steps are the key to finding that balance, so start small, and go from there. Most of all, know your limitations and what works best for you; then decide what really matters, what advice you want to follow, and prioritize.

*Questions 21–27*

*Complete the notes below.*

*Choose **ONE WORD ONLY** from the text for each answer.*

*Write your answers in boxes 21–27 on your answer sheet.*

---

## Achieving a better work–life balance

**How to begin**

- Make a complete **21** ........................................ of things that are not helpful and reduce involvement in them
- Refuse some requests as this can be a useful **22** ........................................ in gaining a better work–life balance

**Things that can help**

- Regular exercise
  - can increase **23** ........................................ significantly
- Sleep
  - insufficient sleep can make people ill
  - avoid focusing on **24** ........................................ in the lead-up to bedtime

**Issues that require attention**

- Those who see other people's **25** ........................................ as more important than their own will suffer
- If the working day is too long, get **26** ........................................ to shorten it occasionally
- People should learn to recognise their own **27** ........................................

---

## SECTION 3   *Questions 28–40*

*Read the text below and answer Questions 28–40.*

# San Francisco's Golden Gate Bridge

A   For several decades in the nineteenth century, there were calls to connect the rapidly growing metropolis of San Francisco to its neighbours across the mile-wide Golden Gate Strait, where San Francisco Bay opens onto the Pacific Ocean. Eventually, in 1919, officials asked the city engineer, Michael O'Shaughnessy, to explore the possibility of building a bridge. He began to consult engineers across the USA about the feasibility of doing so, and the cost. Most doubted whether a bridge could be built at all, or estimated that it would cost $100 million. However, a Chicago-based engineer named Joseph Strauss believed he could complete the project for a modest $25 to $30 million. After his proposal was accepted, Strauss set about convincing the communities on the northern end of the strait that the bridge would be to their benefit, as well as to that of San Francisco. With population centres growing fast, there was severe traffic congestion at the ferry docks, and motor vehicle travel by ferry was fast exceeding capacity.

B   The bridge could not be constructed without the agreement of the US War Department, which owned the land on each side of the Strait and had the power to prevent any harbour construction that might affect shipping traffic. In 1924, San Francisco and Marin counties applied for a permit to build a bridge, and after hearing overwhelming arguments in favour of the project, the Secretary of War agreed.

Despite the economic benefits promised by its supporters, the project met fierce resistance from a number of businesses – particularly ferry companies – and civic leaders. Not only would the bridge be an obstacle to shipping and spoil the bay's natural beauty, they argued, it wouldn't survive the sort of earthquake that had devastated the city in 1906. Eight years of legal actions followed as opponents tried to prevent it from being built.

C   Meanwhile, Strauss's team scrapped their original plans in favour of a suspension span capable of moving more than two feet to each side: this would withstand strong wind far better than a rigid structure. They also planned the two towers, and decided on a paint colour they called 'international orange'.

D   O'Shaughnessy, Strauss and the Secretary to the Mayor of San Francisco believed a special district needed to be created, with responsibility for planning, designing and financing construction. The formation of this district would enable all the counties affected by the bridge to have a say in the proceedings. This happened in 1928, when the California legislature passed an act to establish the Golden Gate Bridge and Highway District, consisting of six counties. In 1930, residents voted on the question of whether to put up their homes, their farms and their business properties as security for a $35 million bond issue to finance construction. The outcome was a large majority in favour.

However, the District struggled to find a financial backer amid the difficulties of the Great Depression, a problem made worse by years of expensive legal proceedings. Now desperate, Strauss personally sought help from the President of Bank of America, who provided a crucial boost by agreeing to buy $6 million in bonds in 1932.

E   Construction began in January 1933, with the excavation of a vast amount of rock to establish the bridge's two anchorages – the structures in the ground that would take the tension from the suspension cables. The crew consisted of virtually anyone capable of withstanding the physical rigours of the job, as out-of-work cab drivers, farmers and clerks lined up for the chance to earn steady wages as ironworkers and cement mixers.

The attempt to build what would be the first bridge support in the open ocean proved an immense challenge. Working from a long framework built out from the San Francisco side, divers plunged to depths of 90 feet through strong currents to blast away rock and remove the debris. The framework was damaged when it was struck by a ship in August 1933 and again during a powerful storm later in the year, setting construction back five months.

F   The two towers were completed in June 1935, and a New Jersey-based company was appointed to handle the on-site construction of the suspension cables. Its engineers had mastered a technique in which individual steel wires were banded together in spools and carried across the length of the bridge on spinning wheels. Given a year to complete the task, they instead finished in just over six months, having spun more than 25,000 individual wires into each massive cable.

The roadway was completed in April 1937, and the bridge officially opened to pedestrians the following month. The next day, President Roosevelt announced its opening via White House telegraph.

G   The Golden Gate has endured as a marvel of modern engineering; its main span was the longest in the world for a suspension bridge until 1981, while its towers made it the tallest bridge of any type until 1993. It withstood a destructive earthquake in 1989 and was closed to traffic only three times in its first 75 years due to weather conditions. Believed to be the most photographed bridge in the world, this landmark was named one of the seven civil engineering wonders of the United States by the American Society of Civil Engineers in 1994.

*Questions 28–35*

The text on pages 47 and 48 has seven sections, **A–G**.

Which section mentions the following?

*Write the correct letter, **A–G**, in boxes 28–35 on your answer sheet.*

**NB** *You may use any letter more than once.*

28   why it was easy to recruit workers to build the bridge

29   a change in the design of the bridge

30   opposition to building the bridge

31   why a bridge was desirable

32   problems with raising funding for the bridge

33   permission being given to build the bridge

34   which records the bridge broke

35   the idea that building a bridge might be impossible

*Questions 36–40*

*Complete the sentences below.*

*Choose **ONE WORD ONLY** from the text for each answer.*

*Write your answers in boxes 36–40 on your answer sheet.*

**36**    Building the bridge required a ....................................... issued by the Secretary of War.

**37**    One objection to building the bridge was that another ...................................... would destroy it.

**38**    Construction was delayed when the framework was damaged by a ship and again by a ............................................ .

**39**    The last part of the bridge to be constructed was the ........................................ .

**40**    The bridge was first used by ........................................ in May 1937.

## WRITING

# WRITING TASK 1

You should spend about 20 minutes on this task.

---

*You have just read an article in an international travel magazine which contained some information about your town that is incorrect.*

*Write a letter to the editor of the magazine. In your letter*

- *correct the information in the article*
- *explain why it is important for the magazine to give correct information*
- *suggest what the magazine should do about this situation*

---

Write at least 150 words.

You do **NOT** need to write any addresses.

Begin your letter as follows:

**Dear Sir or Madam,**

# WRITING TASK 2

You should spend about 40 minutes on this task.

Write about the following topic:

> *Some people think it's better to choose friends who always have the same opinions as them. Other people believe it's good to have friends who sometimes disagree with them.*
>
> *Discuss both these views and give your own opinion.*

Give reasons for your answer and include any relevant examples from your own knowledge or experience.

Write at least 250 words.

## SPEAKING

## PART 1

The examiner asks the candidate about him/herself, his/her home, work or studies and other familiar topics.

**EXAMPLE**

**Social media**

- Which social media websites do you use?
- How much time do you spend on social media sites? [Why/Why not?]
- What kind of information about yourself have you put on social media? [Why/Why not?]
- Is there anything you don't like about social media? [Why?]

## PART 2

**Describe something you liked very much which you bought for your home.**

**You should say:**
    **what you bought**
    **when and where you bought it**
    **why you chose this particular thing**

**and explain why you liked it so much.**

You will have to talk about the topic for one to two minutes. You have one minute to think about what you are going to say. You can make some notes to help you if you wish.

## PART 3

*Discussion topics:*

**Creating a nice home**

*Example questions:*
Why do some people buy lots of things for their home?
Do you think it is very expensive to make a home look nice?
Why don't some people care about how their home looks?

**Different types of home**

*Example questions:*
In what ways is living in a flat/apartment better than living in a house?
Do you think homes will look different in the future?
Do you agree that the kinds of homes people prefer change as they get older?

# Test 3

## SECTION 1    Questions 1–10

Complete the notes below.

Write **ONE WORD AND/OR A NUMBER** for each answer.

---

### Flanders Conference Hotel

*Example*

Customer Services Manager: ......*Angela*...........

**Date available**

- weekend beginning February 4th

**Conference facilities**

- the **1** ............................... room for talks

  (projector and **2** ............................... available)
- area for coffee and an **3** ...............................
- free **4** ............................... throughout
- a standard buffet lunch costs **5** $ ............................... per head

**Accommodation**

- Rooms will cost **6** $ ............................... including breakfast.

**Other facilities**

- The hotel also has a spa and rooftop **7** ............................... .
- There's a free shuttle service to the **8** ............................... .

**Location**

- Wilby Street (quite near the **9** ...............................)
- near to restaurants and many **10** ...............................

---

# SECTION 2     *Questions 11–20*

*Questions 11 and 12*

*Choose **TWO** letters, **A–E**.*

Which **TWO** activities that volunteers do are mentioned?

A    decorating
B    cleaning
C    delivering meals
D    shopping
E    childcare

*Questions 13 and 14*

*Choose **TWO** letters, **A–E**.*

Which **TWO** ways that volunteers can benefit from volunteering are mentioned?

A    learning how to be part of a team
B    having a sense of purpose
C    realising how lucky they are
D    improved ability at time management
E    boosting their employment prospects

*Questions 15–20*

What has each of the following volunteers helped someone to do?

*Choose **SIX** answers from the box and write the correct letter, **A–G**, next to Questions 15–20.*

---

**What volunteers have helped people to do**

A   overcome physical difficulties

B   rediscover skills not used for a long time

C   improve their communication skills

D   solve problems independently

E   escape isolation

F   remember past times

G   start a new hobby

---

**Volunteers**

15   Habib        ....................

16   Consuela     ....................

17   Minh         ....................

18   Tanya        ....................

19   Alexei       ....................

20   Juba         ....................

# SECTION 3      *Questions 21–26*

*Complete the notes below.*

*Write* **ONE WORD AND/OR A NUMBER** *for each answer.*

---

## Background on school marching band

It consists of around **21** ........................................ students.

It is due to play in a **22** ........................................ band competition.

It has been invited to play in the town's **23** ........................................ .

They have listened to a talk by a **24** ........................................ .

Joe will discuss a **25** ........................................ with the band.

Joe hopes the band will attend a **26** ........................................ next month.

---

Questions 27–30

What problem does Joe mention in connection with each of the following band members?

Choose **FOUR** answers from the box and write the correct letter, **A–F**, next to Questions 27–30.

---

**Problems**

A   makes a lot of mistakes in rehearsals

B   keeps making unhelpful suggestions

C   has difficulty with rhythm

D   misses too many rehearsals

E   has a health problem

F   doesn't mix with other students

---

**Band members**

27   flautist          ........................

28   trumpeter        ........................

29   trombonist       ........................

30   percussionist    ........................

## SECTION 4  *Questions 31–40*

*Complete the notes below.*

*Write **ONE WORD AND/OR A NUMBER** for each answer.*

---

### Concerts in university arts festival

**Concert 1**

- Australian composer: Liza Lim
- studied piano and **31** ........................................ before turning to composition
- performers and festivals around the world have given her a lot of commissions
- compositions show a great deal of **32** ........................................ and are drawn from various cultural sources
- her music is very expressive and also **33** ........................................
- festival will include her **34** ........................................ called *The Oresteia*
- Lim described the sounds in *The Oresteia* as **35** ........................................
- British composers: Ralph Vaughan Williams, Frederick Delius

**Concert 2**

- British composers: Benjamin Britten, Judith Weir
- Australian composer: Ross Edwards
- festival will include *The Tower of Remoteness*, inspired by nature
- *The Tower of Remoteness* is performed by piano and **36** ........................................
- compositions include music for children
- celebrates Australia's cultural **37** ........................................

**Concert 3**

- Australian composer: Carl Vine
- played cornet then piano
- studied **38** ........................................ before studying music
- worked in Sydney as a pianist and composer
- became well known as composer of music for **39** ........................................
- festival will include his music for the 1996 **40** ........................................
- British composers: Edward Elgar, Thomas Adès

---

## READING

## SECTION 1    *Questions 1–14*

*Read the text below and answer Questions 1–7.*

# Your guide to entertainment in Westhaven

---

**A    TRAX INDOOR KARTING CENTRE**

Experience the fun and thrills of indoor racing driving in our mini open-topped karts. No experience necessary. Individuals and groups welcome. Refreshments available in new burger bar. Spectators welcome.

All drivers must meet the minimum height requirement of 5 feet (1.52 m), and participate at their own risk.

**Open:** all year daily 10 am to 6 pm (later times by appointment) except
Christmas Eve, Christmas Day, Boxing Day and New Year's Day

**Charges:** from £11 per person

---

**B    WESTHAVEN LIFEBOAT MUSEUM**

The Westhaven Lifeboat Museum is an exciting display illustrating over 150 years of courage – photos with texts of epic rescues, models of lifeboats and video displays. Try our hands-on simulator – take charge of a daring rescue on a stormy sea. Ideal for school groups! A must for all ages. Souvenir shop. No charge for admission but donations welcome.

**Open:** 25th March to 26th October, 10 am to 5 pm
27th October to 2nd January, 10 am to 4 pm

---

**C    STAR LEISURE CENTRE**

Exciting leisure complex with four pools, wave machine, two thrilling flumes, bubble pool, fitness suite, special programme for under-fives, organised holiday activities and much, much more!

**Open**: all year daily

**Charges:** Check our website at *www.starleisure.co.uk* for current rates.

---

## D  LLOYD'S LANES

20 fully computerised ten-pin bowling lanes, amusement area, fast food area, large-screen Sky TV – Lloyd's Lanes is ideal for a whole fun day out!

**Open:** ten-pin bowling daily, 10 am till late – 7 days a week

**Charges:** Monday to Friday 10 am to 6 pm: non-members £3.50; members £2.50

**other times:** non-members £4.50; members £3.75
appropriate footgear essential to protect bowling surfaces
shoe hire £1.00 at all times

## E  WESTHAVEN GOLF CLUB

Beautiful lakeside course; a pleasant, manageable walk through nine challenging holes. 24-bay driving range, suitable in rain, wind or sun; three golf professionals can give affordable coaching. Restaurant: good food served all day. Visitors welcome.

**Open:** all year from 7.30 am to 10 pm

**Charges:** 9 holes £10; 18 holes £15

Questions 1–7

The text on pages 60 and 61 has five advertisements labelled **A–E**.

Which advertisement contains the following information?

*Write the correct letter **A–E** in boxes 1–7 on your answer sheet.*

**NB**  *You may use any letter more than once.*

1    Payment at this venue is optional.

2    Expert instructors are available for lessons.

3    There is a restriction on what you can wear.

4    Some basic information is published in another place.

5    This has particular provision for very young children.

6    It has a feature especially recommended for educational parties.

7    They will open at unscheduled times if you make an arrangement.

*Read the text below and answer Questions 8–14.*

# DO YOU HAVE A MUSIC PROJECT IN MIND THAT MIGHT BENEFIT FROM FUNDING?

Music is wonderfully therapeutic! This is recognised by The Dosoco Foundation, which supports local projects that use music for social good.

The next round of Dosoco grant funding will shortly be open for applications. Grants are available from £700 to £1,000 (for organisations) and up to £300 (for individuals) in the areas of music education (e.g. working with a talented music student with either physical, social or learning disabilities), music access (e.g. a music club for groups that might struggle to start something on their own), music innovation (e.g. using an electronic device such as Raspberry Pi to help disabled people make music) and music therapy (e.g. an idea for using music to support positive mental health).

**Case study**

Dosoco recently awarded a grant to **Alexia Sloane**, a young composer with sight loss, to enable her to attend the sound-and-music summer-school composition course at the Purcell School. Alexia has since gained a place as a composer with the National Youth Orchestra of Great Britain – the first blind composer to be appointed – and has also been awarded the title of Young Composer of the Year. She was the first female composer ever to receive this honour in its ten-year history.

Organisations, families and individuals can apply by completing a simple form. Dosoco can contribute up to 50% towards project costs. Projects must be locally based and must be new ideas for using music to make a positive impact on people's lives where help is really needed.

For more information please visit *www.thedosocofoundation.org*

Questions 8–14

Do the following statements agree with the information given in the text on page 63?

*In boxes 8–14 on your answer sheet, write*

**TRUE**        *if the statement agrees with the information*
**FALSE**        *if the statement contradicts the information*
**NOT GIVEN**   *if there is no information on this*

**8**    You can apply to Dosoco now for grant funding.

**9**    You can apply for a grant that will help to educate a musician.

**10**   Alexia Sloane lost her sight after attending a summer-school composition course.

**11**   Alexia now plays several instruments with the National Youth Orchestra of Great Britain.

**12**   Alexia has received an award for her work in music.

**13**   Applications can be made by filling in an online form.

**14**   In some cases Dosoco will cover the full cost of the project.

**SECTION 2**   *Questions 15–27*

*Read the text below and answer Questions 15–21.*

# Guide to employees on workplace monitoring

## What is workplace monitoring?

Employers have the right to monitor your activities in many situations at work. For example, your activities may be recorded on CCTV cameras, and your letters may be opened and read. In addition, your employer may use an automated software programme to check the emails you receive at work. Phone calls may be listened to and recorded, and the log of websites you use may be checked.

All of these forms of monitoring are covered by data protection law. Data protection law doesn't prevent monitoring in the workplace. However, it does set down rules about the circumstances and the way in which monitoring should be carried out.

Before deciding whether to introduce monitoring, your employer should identify any negative effects the monitoring may have on staff. This is called impact assessment.

## Monitoring electronic communications at work

Your employer can legally monitor your use of electronic communications in the workplace if the monitoring relates to the business and the equipment being monitored is provided partly or wholly for work.

Except in extremely limited circumstances, employers must take reasonable steps to let staff know that monitoring is happening, what is being monitored and why it is necessary.

As long as your employer sticks to these rules, they don't need to get your consent before they monitor your electronic communications, but only if the monitoring is for specific reasons. These may be to establish facts which are relevant to the business or to check standards, for example, listening in to phone calls to assess the quality of your work. Monitoring is also allowed if its purpose is to prevent or detect crime. It may be necessary to make sure electronic systems are operating effectively, for example, to prevent computer viruses entering the system. Your employer is also allowed to listen in to any calls you make to confidential helplines, but in this case he or she is not allowed to record these calls.

*Questions 15–21*

*Complete the notes below.*

*Choose **NO MORE THAN TWO WORDS** from the text for each answer.*

*Write your answers in boxes 15–21 on your answer sheet.*

---

## Guide to employees on workplace monitoring

**Your employer may monitor you at work by checking**

* recordings of your activities

* your letters and **15** .........................................

* your phone calls and which websites you have visited

Rules for monitoring are established by data protection law. This states that employers must carry out a procedure that is known as **16** ........................................ before introducing monitoring.

**In general, monitoring is legal if**

* it relates to the business

* you are using **17** ................................... intended for work

* the worker has been informed

**Monitoring may be used**

* to evaluate the **18** .................................... of your work

* to stop or find out about **19** .......................................

* to stop the possibility of **20** ................................... affecting systems

* to check calls to **21** ................................... (these cannot be recorded)

---

*Read the text below and answer Questions 22–27.*

# International Experience Canada: application process

If you want to travel and work temporarily in Canada as part of International Experience Canada (IEC), your first step is to become a candidate in one or more IEC pools. There are three categories of pool: International Co-op (Internship), Working Holiday and Young Professionals.

To apply, first use our questionnaire to see if you meet the criteria to get into the IEC pools. This should take you about ten minutes. You can find it at *www.cic.gc.ca/ctc-vac/ cometocanada.asp*. After completing this, if you are eligible you will be sent a personal reference code, which you should use to create your online account. At the same time, you should fill in any remaining fields in your profile with the required information, including which IEC pools you want to be in. (Some parts will already have been completed for you.)

If you are sent an invitation to proceed with your application, you will have 10 days to decide whether to accept this or not. If you accept, click the 'Start Application' button. You then have 20 days to complete your application.

For International Co-op and Young Professionals categories, your employer in Canada must pay the compliance fee and inform you of your offer of employment number. (This does not apply to the Working Holiday pool.)

Once you have received this, you should then upload copies of police and medical certificates, if required. If you do not have these, you should upload proof that you have applied for them. You should then pay your participation fee of C$126 online by credit card. (There is an additional payment of C$100 if you are applying for the Working Holiday category.)

Your application will then be assessed. You can apply to withdraw at this stage and will be given a refund if you do this within 56 days. If your application is successful, you will receive a letter of introduction which you can show to Immigration when you enter Canada.

*Questions 22–27*

*Complete the flow-chart below.*

*Choose **ONE WORD AND/OR A NUMBER ONLY** from the text for each answer.*

*Write your answers in boxes 22–27 on your answer sheet.*

# Applying to International Experience Canada

Fill in the online **22** ........................................ to get a personal reference code.

▼

Create your **23** ........................................ and provide the necessary information for the profile in your application.

▼

If sent an invitation, you must accept this within **24** ........................................ . You then have a limited time to **25** ........................................ the application.

▼

Your **26** ........................................ is required to send you an offer of employment number.

▼

Upload copies of any necessary certificates or proof of application.

▼

Make the payment for participation online. You may receive a **27** ........................................ later if you change your mind.

▼

If successful, you will receive a letter of introduction to be shown at Immigration.

**SECTION 3**    *Questions 28–40*

*Read the text below and answer Questions 28–40.*

# RESEARCH ON IMPROVING AGRICULTURAL YIELDS IN AFRICA

*Three programmes are investigating ways of improving agricultural productivity in Africa.*

More than half of the global population growth between now and 2050 is expected to occur in Africa. And more people means a requirement for more food.

Ethiopia, for example, has the largest livestock population in Africa but with a growing population even its 53 million cattle are not enough. And now efforts to develop farming there are bringing a significant health concern. Professor James Wood from the University of Cambridge explains that new breeds that are being introduced are more vulnerable to bovine TB (tuberculosis) than the zebu cattle which were previously reared there. 'This may have health implications for those who work with and live alongside infected cattle, and also raises concerns about transmission to areas which previously had low levels of TB,' he warns.

Wood leads a research programme which is looking at the feasibility of control strategies, including cattle vaccination. The programme brings together veterinary scientists, epidemiologists, geneticists, immunologists and social scientists in eight Ethiopian and UK institutions. 'We need this mix because we are not only asking how effective strategies will be, but also whether farmers will accept them, and what the consequences are for prosperity and wellbeing,' says Wood.

The impact that increasing productivity can have on farmers' livelihoods is not lost on an insect expert at the University of Ghana, Dr Ken Fening, who is working on another food-related research project. Cabbages are not indigenous to Africa but have become a major cash crop for Ghanaian farmers and an important source of income for traders from markets and hotels. 'A good crop can bring in money to buy fertilisers and farm equipment, and also help to pay for healthcare and education for the family,' he says. Recently, however, fields of stunted, yellowing cabbages, their leaves curled and dotted with mould, have become a familiar and devastating sight for the farmers of Ghana.

From his field station base in Kpong, Ghana, Fening works closely with smallholder farmers on pest-control strategies. Two years ago they started reporting that a new disease was attacking their crops. 'It seemed to be associated with massive infestations of pink and green aphids*,' says Fening, 'and from my studies of the way insects interact with many different vegetables, I'm familiar with the types of damage they can cause.'

But farmers were typically seeing the total loss of their crops, and he realised that the devastation couldn't just be caused by sap-sucking insects. Despite no previous reports of viral diseases affecting cabbage crops in Ghana, the symptoms suggested a viral pathogen.

---

\* aphids: small insects which feed by sucking liquid from plants

Together with Cambridge plant biologist Dr John Carr, Fening collected samples of cabbage plants in Ghana showing signs of disease, and also aphids on the diseased plants. Back in Cambridge, Fening used screening techniques including a type of DNA 'fingerprinting' to identify the aphid species, and sophisticated molecular biology methods to try to identify the offending virus.

'Aphids are a common carrier of plant-infecting viruses,' explains Carr. 'The "usual suspects" are turnip mosaic virus and cauliflower mosaic virus, which affect cabbages in Europe and the US.'

'We found that two different species of aphids, pink and green, were generally found on the diseased cabbages,' says Fening. 'It turned out this was the first record of the green aphid species ever being seen in Ghana.' The pink aphid was identified as *Myzus persicae* (Sulzer).

What's more, the virus was not what they expected, and work is now ongoing to identify the culprit. The sooner it can be characterised, the sooner sustainable crop protection strategies can be developed to prevent further spread of the disease not only in Ghana, but also in other countries in the region.

Another researcher who hopes that eradication strategies will be the outcome of her research project is Dr Theresa Manful. Like Fening, she is a researcher at the University of Ghana. She has been working with Cambridge biochemist Professor Mark Carrington on a disease known as trypanosomiasis.

'This is a major constraint to cattle rearing in Africa,' she explains. 'Although trypanosomiasis is also a disease of humans, the number of cases is low, and the more serious concerns about the disease relate to the economic impact on agricultural production.'

The parasite that causes the disease is carried by the tsetse fly, which colonises vast swathes of sub-Saharan Africa. Carrington says that a lot is now known about the parasite's molecular mechanisms, in particular the way it evades the immune system of the animal acting as its host by altering the proteins in its coat so as to remain 'invisible'. 'But then when you look at the effect on large animals, you realise that there is almost nothing known about the dynamics of an infection, and even whether an infection acquired at an early age persists for its lifetime,' he says. So Manful and Carrington set about testing cattle in Ghana. They discovered that nearly all were infected most of the time.

For Manful, one of the important gains has been the ability to expand the research in Ghana: 'I now have a fully functional lab and can do DNA extraction and analysis in Ghana – I don't have to bring samples to Cambridge. We are teaching students from five Ghanaian institutions the diagnostic methods.'

'Agriculture faces increasing challenges,' adds Carr. 'Bioscience is playing a crucial part in developing ways to mitigate pest impact and reduce the spread of parasites. We want to ensure not only that every harvest is successful, but also that it's maximally successful.'

*Questions 28–32*

*Choose the correct letter, **A**, **B**, **C** or **D**.*

*Write the correct letter in boxes 28–32 on your answer sheet.*

**28**  What is the main problem faced by cattle farmers in Ethiopia, according to Professor Wood?

    **A**  TB is being transmitted from people to cattle.
    **B**  New breeds of cattle have led to an increase in TB.
    **C**  The traditional breeds of cattle are being affected by TB.
    **D**  TB has spread into places where it was previously unknown.

**29**  When discussing the cultivation of cabbages in Ghana, the writer says that this crop

    **A**  was introduced from outside Africa.
    **B**  is not eaten much by local people.
    **C**  is not grown correctly by many farmers.
    **D**  requires the use of fertiliser and special equipment.

**30**  Fening believed that the new disease destroying cabbages was

    **A**  caused by overuse of pesticides.
    **B**  also affecting other locally grown vegetables.
    **C**  linked to insect attacks on these vegetables.
    **D**  connected with the development of new insect breeds.

**31**  Fening first suspected that the cabbage disease was caused by a virus because

    **A**  evidence of viral disease could be seen on the cabbage leaves.
    **B**  pink and green aphids did not commonly attack cabbages.
    **C**  viral diseases affecting vegetables had occurred elsewhere in Africa.
    **D**  aphids would not have caused so much damage to the crops.

**32**  When doing further research in Cambridge, Fening and Carr discovered that

    **A**  the virus was unfamiliar to them.
    **B**  two different viruses were present.
    **C**  the aphids' DNA was more complex than expected.
    **D**  one aphid was more harmful than the other.

*Questions 33–36*

*Look at the following statements (Questions 33–36) and the list of researchers below.*

*Match each statement with the correct researcher, **A–E**.*

*Write the correct letter, **A–E**, in boxes 33–36 on your answer sheet.*

**NB** *You may use any letter more than once.*

**33**  A particular crop may make an important contribution to the local economy in one African country.

**34**  Tests will be carried out by local people in the country where the research is focused.

**35**  Different specialists must work together to ensure the success of a programme.

**36**  One type of insect attacking plants in Ghana was previously unknown there.

---

**List of Researchers**

**A**    James Wood

**B**    Ken Fening

**C**    John Carr

**D**    Theresa Manful

**E**    Mark Carrington

---

*Questions 37–40*

*Complete the summary below.*

*Choose* **NO MORE THAN TWO WORDS** *from the text for each answer.*

*Write your answers in boxes 37–40 on your answer sheet.*

## Trypanosomiasis

Trypanosomiasis is a disease caused by a parasite which is spread by an insect called the **37** ........................................... . The parasite can remain unaffected by the host's **38** ........................................ because it is able to change the **39** ....................................... on its outer covering. It is uncommon among humans but has been found to affect most **40** ........................................ in Ghana.

## WRITING

# WRITING TASK 1

You should spend about 20 minutes on this task.

---

*You recently did a short cookery course. The cookery school has asked for your feedback on this course.*

*Write a letter to the course director at the cookery school. In your letter*

- *describe what you enjoyed about the course*
- *say how much cooking you've done since the course*
- *suggest another cookery course you'd like the school to offer*

---

Write at least 150 words.

You do **NOT** need to write any addresses.

Begin your letter as follows:

**Dear Sir or Madam,**

# WRITING TASK 2

You should spend about 40 minutes on this task.

Write about the following topic:

> **Some people say the main way to be happy in life is to have a lot of money.**
>
> **How might having a lot of money make people happy?**
>
> **What other things in life can make people happy?**

Give reasons for your answer and include any relevant examples from your own knowledge or experience.

Write at least 250 words.

# SPEAKING

## PART 1

The examiner asks the candidate about him/herself, his/her home, work or studies and other familiar topics.

### EXAMPLE

**Neighbours**

- How often do you see your neighbours? [Why/Why not?]
- Do you invite your neighbours to your home? [Why/Why not?]
- Do you think you are a good neighbour? [Why/Why not?]
- Has a neighbour ever helped you? [Why/Why not?]

## PART 2

**Describe a very difficult task that you succeeded in doing as part of your work or studies.**

**You should say:**
> **what task you did**
> **why this task was very difficult**
> **how you worked on this task**

**and explain how you felt when you had successfully completed this task.**

You will have to talk about the topic for one to two minutes. You have one minute to think about what you are going to say. You can make some notes to help you if you wish.

## PART 3

*Discussion topics:*

**Difficult jobs**

*Example questions:*
What are the most difficult jobs that people do?
Why do you think some people choose to do difficult jobs?
Do you agree or disagree that all jobs are difficult sometimes?

**Personal and career success**

*Example questions:*
How important is it for everyone to have a goal in their personal life?
Is it always necessary to work hard in order to achieve career success?
Do you think that successful people are always happy people?

# Test 4

**SECTION 1**   *Questions 1–10*

*Questions 1–7*

*Complete the notes below.*

*Write **ONE WORD AND/OR A NUMBER** for each answer.*

---

## Enquiry about booking hotel room for event

*Example*

Andrew is the ............*Events*............ Manager

**Rooms**

Adelphi Room
    number of people who can sit down to eat: **1** ..........................................
    has a gallery suitable for musicians
    can go out and see the **2** ................................. in pots on the terrace
    terrace has a view of a <u>group</u> of **3** ...............................

Carlton Room
    number of people who can sit down to eat: 110
    has a **4** ...............................
    view of the lake

**Options**

Master of Ceremonies:
    can give a **5** ............................... while people are eating
    will provide **6** ............................... if there are any problems

Accommodation:
    in hotel rooms or **7** ...............................

---

*Questions 8–10*

What is said about using each of the following hotel facilities?

*Choose **THREE** answers from the box and write the correct letter, **A, B** or **C**, next to
Questions 8–10.*

**Availability**

A  included in cost of hiring room

B  available at extra charge

C  not available

**Hotel facilities**

8  outdoor swimming pool  .....................

9  gym  .....................

10  tennis courts  .....................

# SECTION 2    *Questions 11–20*

*Questions 11–16*

What information does the speaker give about each of the following excursions?

*Choose **SIX** answers from the box and write the correct letter, **A–H**, next to Questions 11–16.*

| | Information |
|---|---|
| A | all downhill |
| B | suitable for beginners |
| C | only in good weather |
| D | food included |
| E | no charge |
| F | swimming possible |
| G | fully booked today |
| H | transport not included |

**Excursions**

| | | |
|---|---|---|
| 11 | dolphin watching | .................... |
| 12 | forest walk | .................... |
| 13 | cycle trip | .................... |
| 14 | local craft tour | .................... |
| 15 | observatory trip | .................... |
| 16 | horse riding | .................... |

Questions 17 and 18

Choose **TWO** letters, **A–E**.

Which **TWO** things does the speaker say about the attraction called *Musical Favourites*?

    **A**    You pay extra for drinks.

    **B**    You must book it in advance.

    **C**    You get a reduction if you buy two tickets.

    **D**    You can meet the performers.

    **E**    You can take part in the show.

Questions 19 and 20

Choose **TWO** letters, **A–E**.

Which **TWO** things does the speaker say about the *Castle Feast*?

    **A**    Visitors can dance after the meal.

    **B**    There is a choice of food.

    **C**    Visitors wear historical costume.

    **D**    Knives and forks are not used.

    **E**    The entertainment includes horse races.

# SECTION 3    *Questions 21–30*

*Questions 21–25*

*Choose the correct letter, **A**, **B** or **C**.*

21  What does Trevor find interesting about the purpose of children's literature?

    **A**    the fact that authors may not realise what values they're teaching
    **B**    the fact that literature can be entertaining and educational at the same time
    **C**    the fact that adults expect children to imitate characters in literature

22  Trevor says the module about the purpose of children's literature made him

    **A**    analyse some of the stories that his niece reads.
    **B**    wonder how far popularity reflects good quality.
    **C**    decide to start writing some children's stories.

23  Stephanie is interested in the Pictures module because

    **A**    she intends to become an illustrator.
    **B**    she can remember beautiful illustrations from her childhood.
    **C**    she believes illustrations are more important than words.

24  Trevor and Stephanie agree that comics

    **A**    are inferior to books.
    **B**    have the potential for being useful.
    **C**    discourage children from using their imagination.

25  With regard to books aimed at only boys or only girls, Trevor was surprised

    **A**    how long the distinction had gone unquestioned.
    **B**    how few books were aimed at both girls and boys.
    **C**    how many children enjoyed books intended for the opposite sex.

*Questions 26–30*

What comment is made about each of these stories?

*Choose* **FIVE** *answers from the box and write the correct letter,* **A–G**, *next to Questions 26–30.*

| Comments |
| --- |
| **A**   translated into many other languages |
| **B**   hard to read |
| **C**   inspired a work in a different area of art |
| **D**   more popular than the author's other works |
| **E**   original title refers to another book |
| **F**   started a new genre |
| **G**   unlikely topic |

**Stories**

**26**   Perrault's fairy tales   .....................

**27**   *The Swiss Family Robinson*   .....................

**28**   *The Nutcracker and The Mouse King*   .....................

**29**   *The Lord of the Rings*   .....................

**30**   *War Horse*   .....................

# SECTION 4    *Questions 31–40*

*Complete the notes below.*

*Write **ONE WORD ONLY** for each answer.*

---

## The hunt for sunken settlements and ancient shipwrecks

**ATLIT-YAM**

- was a village on coast of eastern Mediterranean
- thrived until about 7,000 BC
- stone homes had a courtyard
- had a semicircle of large stones round a **31** ....................................
- cause of destruction unknown – now under the sea
- biggest settlement from the prehistoric period found on the seabed
- research carried out into structures, **32** ................................... and human remains

**TRADITIONAL AUTONOMOUS UNDERWATER VEHICLES (AUVs)**

- used in the oil industry, e.g. to make **33** ...................................
- problems: they were expensive and **34** ...................................

**LATEST AUVs**

- much easier to use, relatively cheap, sophisticated

**Tests:**

- Marzamemi, Sicily: found ancient Roman ships carrying architectural elements made of **35** ...................................

**Underwater internet:**

- **36** ................................... is used for short distance communication, acoustic waves for long distance
- plans for communication with researchers by satellite
- AUV can send data to another AUV that has better **37** ..................................., for example

**Planned research in Gulf of Baratti:**

- to find out more about wrecks of ancient Roman ships, including
  - one carrying **38** ................................... supplies; tablets may have been used for cleaning the **39** ...................................
  - others carrying containers of olive oil or **40** ...................................

---

**READING**

## SECTION 1    *Questions 1–14*

*Read the text below and answer Questions 1–8.*

# The best travel wallets

*Keep all your bank cards, documents, passports and ID in one of these convenient carriers, which have been selected by Becca Meier.*

**A    Kipling Travel Doc Travel Document Holder**

This zip-around wallet comes in five different patterns and is made of nylon. It also has a space where users can put a pen, pockets for cards, an ID window and a pocket for change.

**B    Lifeventure Mini Travel Document Wallet**

This is a waterproof wallet, which uses anti-RFID (radio frequency identification) material so your financial details will be safe. It is black with smart sky-blue finishing touches and has a small internal compartment, a smartphone pocket and an external pocket. It can fit two passports.

**C    Cath Kidston Breton Stripe**

A wallet so slim it could easily pass for a small notebook. The inside compartment labels identifying each separate section all have silver lettering on them. The wallet has a special coating which makes it easy to wipe anything like sand off.

**D    Ted Baker Voyager's Travel Wallet**

This wallet comes in smooth black leather, and is no bigger than a passport, but roomy enough for any insurance documents or flight tickets. A small navy-blue pen is supplied inside.

**E    Radley Abbey Travel Wallet**

This plain travel wallet opens up to reveal pockets in various colours labelled 'cards', 'passport' and 'tickets', as well as others left blank for extras. It comes in a handy drawstring bag.

**F    Gotravel Organiser**

The black wallet features seven slip-in card compartments, two small interior zip pockets and a load of other slip-in compartments. It can fit at least four passports.

**G    Gotravel Glo Travel Wallet**

This is a simple, very reasonably priced wallet. It is made of PVC plastic and will suit those who like a wallet that is easy to spot. It comes in a range of bright colours with a white holiday-related design on the front. It has five compartments that can fit a passport with other cards/tickets.

*Questions 1–8*

*Look at the seven reviews of travel wallets, **A–G**, on page 84.*

For which travel wallet are the following statements true?

*Write the correct letter, **A–G**, in boxes 1–8 on your answer sheet.*

**NB** *You may use any letter more than once.*

1  This wallet will suit people who prefer natural materials.

2  Users of this wallet do not need to worry about taking it out in the rain.

3  Parts of the inside of this wallet have categories printed on them in one colour.

4  This wallet would suit someone who needs to keep several passports together.

5  Something is provided for writing.

6  This will suit people who want to be able to find their document wallet easily in their luggage.

7  Something to keep this wallet in is provided.

8  This wallet has been specially made to prevent people detecting the numbers on any bank cards, etc. inside it.

*Read the text below and answer Questions 9–14.*

# UK rail services – how do I claim for my delayed train?

Generally, if you have been delayed on a train journey, you may be able to claim compensation, but train companies all have different rules, so it can be confusing to work out what you're entitled to. The type of delay you can claim for depends on whether the train company runs a Delay Repay scheme or a less generous, older-style scheme.

Delay Repay is a train operator scheme to compensate passengers when trains are late, and the train company will pay out even if it was not responsible for the delay. The scheme varies between companies, but up to 2016 most paid 50 percent of the single ticket cost for 30 minutes' delay and 100 percent for an hour. On the London Underground, you get a full refund for 15-minute delays.

Companies that do not use Delay Repay and still use the older scheme will not usually pay compensation if the problem is considered to be out of their control. But it is still worth asking them for compensation, as some may pay out. You are unlikely to get compensation for a delay if any of the following occur:

- Accidents involving people getting onto the line illegally
- Gas leaks or fires in buildings next to the line which were not caused by a train company
- Line closures at the request of the emergency services
- Exceptionally severe weather conditions
- Strike action

National Rail Conditions of Travel state that you are entitled to compensation in the same form that you paid for the ticket. Some train companies are still paying using rail vouchers, which they are allowed to do if you do not ask for a cash refund.

Since 2016, rail passengers have acquired further rights for compensation through the Consumer Rights Act. This means that passengers could now be eligible for compensation due to: a severely overcrowded train with too few carriages available; a consistently late running service; and a service that is delayed for less than the time limit that applied under existing compensation schemes.

However, in order to exercise their rights beyond the existing compensation schemes, for instance Delay Repay, and where the train operating company refuses to compensate despite letters threatening court action, passengers may need to bring their claims to a court of law.

*Questions 9–14*

Do the following statements agree with the information given in the text on page 86?

*In boxes 9–14 on your answer sheet, write*

>  **TRUE**        *if the statement agrees with the information*
>  **FALSE**       *if the statement contradicts the information*
>  **NOT GIVEN**   *if there is no information on this*

**9**   The system for claiming compensation varies from one company to another.

**10**  Under Delay Repay, a train company will only provide compensation if it caused the delay.

**11**  Under Delay Repay, underground and other train companies give exactly the same amounts of money in compensation.

**12**  An increasing number of train companies are willing to pay compensation for problems they are not responsible for.

**13**  It is doubtful whether companies using the older scheme will provide compensation if a delay is caused by a strike.

**14**  Passengers may receive compensation in the form of a train voucher if they forget to request cash.

## SECTION 2　　*Questions 15–27*

*Read the text below and answer Questions 15–19.*

# Vacancy for food preparation assistant

Durrant House plc runs restaurants and cafés as concessions in airports, train stations and other busy environments around the country. We currently have a vacancy for a food preparation assistant in our restaurant at Locksley Stadium, serving football fans and concert-goers before, during and after events. In addition, we cater for private parties several times a week. If you have relevant experience and a passion for preparing food to a very high standard, we'll be delighted to hear from you. You must be able to multitask and to work in a fast-paced environment. It goes without saying that working as an effective and supportive member of a team is essential, so you need to be happy in this type of work.

The role includes the usual responsibilities, such as treating hygiene as your number one priority, cleaning work areas, and doing whatever is required to provide food of excellent quality. The person appointed will carry out a range of tasks, including ensuring all raw food items are fresh, preparing vegetables to be cooked, making sure frozen food products are used in rotation, and throwing away any food products that are near or have passed their expiry date. He or she will be required to familiarise themselves with the storage system, so as to put food product supplies in the proper place and retrieve them in the right order. In particular, we are looking for someone with skill at baking, to play a large role in the production of pies and cakes.

Given the nature of the venue, working hours vary from week to week, depending on the events being held, and will often involve starting early in the morning or finishing late at night. You can expect to work an average of around 18 hours a week, although this cannot be guaranteed. You will also have the opportunity to work in another of our sites for one or two days a week, or for longer periods, and will be paid for ten days of holidays a year. Training will be provided in food safety.

If this sounds like the job for you, please contact Jo Simmons at simmons.j@durrant-house.com.

*Questions 15–19*

*Complete the notes below.*

*Choose ONE WORD ONLY from the text for each answer.*

*Write your answers in boxes 15–19 on your answer sheet.*

---

# Vacancy for food preparation assistant

**Location of restaurant:** in a **15** ......................................

**Requirements:**

• relevant experience

• ability to multitask

• must enjoy working in a **16** ......................................

**Responsibilities include:**

• maintaining high standards of **17** ...................................... and quality

• checking the freshness of raw food

• ensuring no food is used after its expiry date

• learning the procedure for the **18** ...................................... of food

• doing a considerable amount of the baking

**Conditions:**

• working hours are not **19** ......................................

• payment is made for holidays

---

*Read the text below and answer Questions 20–27.*

# Setting up a business partnership in the UK

Two or more people can go into business together by setting up either a limited company or a partnership. A partnership is the easier way to get started, and simply links two or more people together in a simple business structure. Unlike a limited company, a partnership doesn't have a separate legal status. The partners are usually self-employed individuals, although a limited company counts as a 'legal person' and can also be a partner.

In a partnership, you and your partner or partners personally share responsibility for your business. This means, among other things, that if your business cannot afford to pay its debts, you must pay them yourselves. Again, this is not the case with a limited company. Partners share the business's profits, and each partner pays tax on their share.

When you set up a business partnership you need to choose a name. You can trade under your own names, for example, 'Smith and Jones', or you can choose another name for your business. You don't need to register your name. However, you should register your name as a trademark if you want to stop people from trading under your business name.

Business partnership names must not include 'limited', 'Ltd', 'limited liability partnership', 'LLP', 'public limited company' or 'plc', be offensive, or be the same as an existing trademark. Your name also can't suggest a connection with government or local authorities, unless you get permission. There is no central database of partnership names in the UK, so to avoid using the same name as another business, it is advisable to search on the internet for the name you are considering.

You must include all the partners' names and the business name (if you have one) on official paperwork, for example invoices.

You must choose a 'nominated partner' who is responsible for registering your partnership with HM Revenue and Customs (HMRC), the government department responsible for the collection of taxes. This person is responsible for managing the partnership's tax returns and keeping business records. Alternatively, you can appoint an agent to deal with HMRC on your behalf.

All partners need to register with HMRC separately and send their own tax returns as individuals.

You must register by 5 October in your business's second tax year, or you could be charged a penalty.

You must also register for VAT if your VAT taxable turnover is more than £85,000. You can choose to register if it's below this, for example to reclaim VAT on business supplies.

*Questions 20–27*

*Complete the sentences below.*

*Choose **ONE WORD ONLY** from the text for each answer.*

*Write your answers in boxes 20–27 on your answer sheet.*

**20**  A partnership is different from a limited company in not having its own ............................................ as a legal body.

**21**  The partners are personally responsible for paying all the partnership's ............................................ .

**22**  The partnership's ............................................ are divided between the partners.

**23**  Registering the partnership's name prevents others from using that name when ............................................ .

**24**  The best way to find out if a name is already in use is to use the ............................................ .

**25**  The names of the partners and the partnership must appear on ............................................ and other documents.

**26**  You must have a nominated partner, or someone to act as your ............................................ , for all contact with HMRC.

**27**  You will have to pay a ............................................ if you miss the deadline for registering the partnership.

## SECTION 3    *Questions 28–40*

*Read the text below and answer Questions 28–40.*

# THE ROLE OF THE SWISS POSTBUS

*Switzerland's postbuses are much more than just a means of
public transportation.*

The Swiss PostBus Limited is the largest of the country's 78 coach companies. Administered by the Motor Services Department of the Post Office, it carries over 120 million passengers each year and is carefully integrated with other public transport services: trains, boats and mountain cableways. The Swiss transportation system resembles a tree, with the larger branches representing federal and private railways, the smaller branches being the coaches, and the twigs being the urban transit operators running trams, city buses, boats, chairlifts and so on. But the trunk that holds the tree together is the vast postbus network, without which the whole network would not function.

There isn't an inhabited place in Switzerland that cannot be reached by some sort of public transport. Federal law and the Swiss Constitution stipulate that every village with a population greater than 40 is entitled to regular bus services. The frequency of these services is directly related to population density. Timetables are put together four years in advance, and seldom change. If a new route is to be introduced, the population of the area affected is invited to vote in a referendum.

At times, postbuses are the main – sometimes the only – links between settlements. These coaches, often with a trailer in tow to increase their capacity, are a common sight in high-altitude regions, and their signature sound – part of Rossini's *William Tell Overture*, played by the drivers on three-tone post horns with electrical compressors at every road turn – is one of the most familiar Swiss sounds.

The three-tone horns can still be used to 'talk' to post offices (and each other) from a distance. By altering the combination of the tones, a driver can announce 'departure of post', 'arrival of post', 'arrival of special post', and so on – so much more romantic and often more reliable than radio or mobile phones. This musical 'language' started in the mid-nineteenth century, when the coach drivers could also blow their horns a certain number of times on approaching the station to indicate the number of horses needing to be fed, giving the stationmaster time to prepare the fodder.

The postbus history goes back to 1849, when the Swiss postal service was made a monopoly. The role of today's modern yellow buses was, back then, played by horse-drawn carriages (or in winter by sleighs, in order to travel on snow), which were the same colour. By 1914, eight years after the first motor coaches were introduced, there were still 2,500 horses, 2,231 coaches (or carriages) and 1,059 sleighs in service.

After the First World War, Swiss Post bought a fleet of decommissioned military trucks which were converted into postbuses, but it was not until 1961 that the last horse-drawn coach was replaced with a motorised version.

Today, the Swiss Post Office boasts one of the world's most advanced coach fleets, including fuel-cell models and the world's first driverless bus. This was launched in 2015 in the town of Sion, the capital of the canton of Valais, one of the 26 cantons, or administrative regions, that make up the country.

Postbuses often go to places that other means of transport cannot reach. Most of the drivers therefore see themselves as educators and tour guides. Although it's not in their job description, they're likely to point out the sights – waterfalls, gorges, and so on – and are always ready to pull over for a photo opportunity.

Switzerland's longest postbus journey, and one of the highest, crosses four mountain passes – an eight-hour trip undertaken by a single postbus. The route goes through several cantons; two languages (German and Italian); all four seasons – from burning sunshine to showers and heavy snowfalls; and countless places of interest. One of the passes, the Gotthard, is often described as 'the People's Road', probably because it connects the German-speaking canton of Uri with Italian-speaking Ticino. Like Switzerland itself, postbuses 'speak' all four state languages: German, French, Italian and Romansh – and,

by law, their automated intercom announcements are given in the language of whichever canton the bus is currently passing through.

Irrespective of their previous driving experience, drivers undergo lots of training. During the first year, they have to drive postbuses under the supervision of a more experienced driver. Only after two years of safe driving in the valleys can they be pronounced ready for a mountain bus.

Some routes are not at all busy, with the bus often carrying just two or three passengers at a time. But for most people living in small mountain villages, the postbus is of the utmost importance. It not only carries the villagers to town and back, it takes village children to and from school, delivers mail, transports milk from the village farms down to the valley, collects rubbish from the village (Swiss laws do not allow dumping anywhere in the mountains), and brings building materials to households. It takes elderly villagers to shops and carries their shopping up the hill to their homes. More a friend than just a means of transportation, for the dwellers of mountain villages the postbus is an essential part of life.

Questions 28–32

*Choose the correct letter, **A**, **B**, **C** or **D**.*

*Write the correct letter in boxes 28–32 on your answer sheet.*

28 When comparing the Swiss transportation system to a tree, the writer emphasises

    **A**   the size of the postbus system.
    **B**   how competitive the postbus system is.
    **C**   how important the postbus system is.
    **D**   the threat to the postbus system.

29 What is said about bus services in the second paragraph?

    **A**   Villages have the chance to request more buses every four years.
    **B**   New routes are often introduced to reflect an increase in population.
    **C**   Bus timetables tend to change every four years.
    **D**   The number of buses that call at a village depends on how many people live there.

30 According to the fourth paragraph, what were three-tone horns first used to indicate?

    **A**   how many coach horses required food
    **B**   how long the bus would stay at the station
    **C**   how many passengers wanted a meal
    **D**   how soon the bus would arrive at the station

31 What point does the writer make about the postbus drivers?

    **A**   Many choose to give passengers information about the surroundings.
    **B**   Most are proud of driving buses to places without other forms of transport.
    **C**   They are required to inform passengers about the sights seen from the bus.
    **D**   They are not allowed to stop for passengers to take photographs.

32 What is said about the buses' automated announcements?

    **A**   They are given in the language of the bus's starting point.
    **B**   The language they are given in depends on where the bus is at the time.
    **C**   They are always given in all the four languages of Switzerland.
    **D**   The language they are given in depends on the bus's destination.

*Questions 33–40*

Do the following statements agree with the information given in the text on pages 92 and 93?

*In boxes 33–40 on your answer sheet, write*

| | |
|---|---|
| **TRUE** | *if the statement agrees with the information* |
| **FALSE** | *if the statement contradicts the information* |
| **NOT GIVEN** | *if there is no information on this* |

**33** Some postbuses after the First World War were originally army vehicles.

**34** The number of driverless buses has increased steadily since 2015.

**35** On the longest postbus route in Switzerland, passengers have to change buses.

**36** The weather on the longest postbus route is likely to include extreme weather conditions.

**37** There is a widely used nickname for part of the longest route used by postbuses.

**38** Bus drivers' training can be shortened if they have driven buses before joining PostBus.

**39** In some villages most passengers are school children.

**40** Buses carry only rubbish that can be recycled.

# WRITING

## WRITING TASK 1

You should spend about 20 minutes on this task.

---

*You recently went to a concert and thought one of the singers was very good. You want to tell him how you feel.*

*Write a letter to the singer. In your letter*
- *say how you feel about his performance*
- *give details of your musical activities*
- *explain how you would like him to help you with your musical activities*

---

Write at least 150 words.

You do **NOT** need to write any addresses.

Begin your letter as follows:

Dear ........................................ ,

# WRITING TASK 2

You should spend about 40 minutes on this task.

Write about the following topic:

> **Many people work long hours, leaving very little time for leisure activities.**
>
> **Does this situation have more advantages or more disadvantages?**

Give reasons for your answer and include any relevant examples from your own knowledge or experience.

Write at least 250 words.

# SPEAKING

## PART 1

The examiner asks the candidate about him/herself, his/her home, work or studies and other familiar topics.

### EXAMPLE

**Your neighbourhood**

- Do you like the neighbourhood you live in? [Why/Why not?]
- What do you do in your neighbourhood in your free time? [Why/Why not?]
- What new things would you like to have in your neighbourhood? [Why/Why not?]
- Would you like to live in another neighbourhood in your town or city? [Why/Why not?]

## PART 2

**Describe a website you have bought something from.**

**You should say:**
    **what the website is**
    **what you bought from this website**
    **how satisfied you were with what you bought**

**and explain what you liked and disliked about using this website.**

You will have to talk about the topic for one to two minutes. You have one minute to think about what you are going to say. You can make some notes to help you if you wish.

## PART 3

*Discussion topics:*

**Shopping online**

*Example questions:*
What kinds of things do people in your country often buy from online shops?
Why has online shopping become so popular in many countries?
What are some possible disadvantages of buying things from online shops?

**Online retail businesses**

*Example questions:*
Do you agree that the prices of all goods should be lower on internet shopping sites than in shops?
Will large shopping malls continue to be popular, despite the growth of internet shopping?
Do you think that some businesses (e.g. banks and travel agents) will only operate online in the future?

# Audioscripts

## SECTION 1

| OFFICER: | Good morning. What can I do for you? | |
|---|---|---|
| LOUISE: | I want to report a theft. I had some things stolen out of my bag yesterday. | |
| OFFICER: | I'm sorry to hear that. Right, so I'll need to take a few details. Can I start with your name? | |
| LOUISE: | Louise <u>Taylor</u>. | *Example* |
| OFFICER: | OK, thank you. And are you resident in the UK? | |
| LOUISE: | No, I'm actually <u>Canadian</u>, though my mother was British. | Q1 |
| OFFICER: | And your date of birth? | |
| LOUISE: | December 14th, 1977. | |
| OFFICER: | So you're just visiting this country? | |
| LOUISE: | That's right. I come over most summers on business. I'm an interior designer and I come over to buy old <u>furniture</u>, antiques you know. There are some really lovely things around here, but you need to get out to the small towns. I've had a really good trip this year, until this happened. | Q2 |
| OFFICER: | OK. So you've been here quite a while? | |
| LOUISE: | Yes, I'm here for two months. I go back next week. | |
| OFFICER: | So may I ask where you're staying now? | |
| LOUISE: | Well at present I've got a place at <u>Park</u> Apartments, that's on King Street. I was staying at the Riverside Apartments on the same street, but the apartment there was only available for six weeks so I had to find another one. | Q3 |
| OFFICER: | OK. And the apartment number? | |
| LOUISE: | Fifteen. | |
| LOUISE: | Right. | |

---

| OFFICER: | Now, I need to take some details of the theft. So you said you had some things stolen out of your bag? | |
|---|---|---|
| LOUISE: | That's right. | |
| OFFICER: | And were you actually carrying the bag when the theft took place? | |
| LOUISE: | Yes. I really can't understand it. I had my backpack on. And I went into a supermarket to buy a few things and when I opened it up my wallet wasn't there. | |
| OFFICER: | And what did your wallet have in it? | |
| LOUISE: | Well, fortunately I don't keep my credit cards in that wallet – I keep them with my passport in an inside compartment in my backpack. But there was quite a bit of cash there … about £<u>250</u> sterling, I should think. I withdrew £300 from my account yesterday, but I did a bit of shopping, so I must have already spent about £50 of that. | Q4 |
| OFFICER: | OK. | |
| LOUISE: | At first I thought, oh I must have left the wallet back in the apartment, but then I realised my <u>phone</u> had gone as well. It was only a week old, and that's when I realised I'd been robbed. Anyway at least they didn't take the keys to my rental car. | Q5 |

| OFFICER: | Yes. So you say the theft occurred yesterday? | |
|---|---|---|
| LOUISE: | Yes. | |
| OFFICER: | So that was <u>September the tenth</u>. And do you have any idea at all of where or when the things might possibly have been stolen? | Q6 |
| LOUISE: | Well at first I couldn't believe it because the bag had been on my back ever since I left the apartment after lunch. It's just a small backpack, but I generally use it when I'm travelling because it seems safer than a handbag. Anyway, I met up with a friend, and we spent a couple of hours in the <u>museum</u>. But I do remember that as we were leaving there, at about 4 o'clock, a group of young boys ran up to us, and they were really crowding round us, and they were asking us what <u>time</u> it was, then all of a sudden they ran off. | Q7<br>Q8 |
| OFFICER: | Can you remember anything about them? | |
| LOUISE: | The one who did most of the talking was wearing a T-shirt with a picture of something … let's see … a tiger. | |
| OFFICER: | Right. Any idea of how old he might have been? | |
| LOUISE: | Around twelve years old? | |
| OFFICER: | And can you remember anything else about his appearance? | |
| LOUISE: | Not much. He was quite thin … | |
| OFFICER: | Colour of hair? | |
| LOUISE: | I do remember that – he was <u>blond</u>. All the others were dark-haired. | Q9 |
| OFFICER: | And any details of the others? | |
| LOUISE: | Not really. They came and went so quickly. | |
| OFFICER: | Right. So what I'm going to do now is give you a crime reference number so you can contact your insurance company. So this is ten digits: <u>87954 82361</u>. | Q10 |
| LOUISE: | Thank you. So should I … | |

# SECTION 2

Good morning everyone. My name's Janet Parker and I'm the human resources manager. We're very happy to welcome you to your new apprenticeship. I hope that the next six months will be a positive and enjoyable experience for you.

I'd like to start with some general advice about being an apprentice. Most of you have very little or no experience of working for a big organisation and the first week or so may be quite challenging. There will be a lot of new information to take in but don't worry too much about trying to remember everything. The important thing is to <u>check with someone if you're not sure what to</u> **Q11** <u>do</u> – you'll find your supervisor is very approachable and won't mind explaining things or helping you out. You're here to learn so make the most of that opportunity. You'll be spending time in different departments during your first week so make an effort to <u>talk to as many people as</u> **Q12** <u>possible</u> about their work – you'll make some new friends and find out lots of useful information.

As well as having a supervisor, you'll each be assigned a mentor. This person will be someone who's recently completed an apprenticeship and you'll meet with them on a weekly basis. Their role is to provide help and support throughout your apprenticeship. Of course, this doesn't mean they'll actually do any of your work for you – instead they'll be asking you about <u>what</u> **Q13** <u>goals you've achieved so far</u>, as well as helping you to <u>identify any areas for improvement</u>. You **Q14** can also <u>discuss your more long-term ambitions</u> with them as well.

Now I just want to run through a few company policies for our apprenticeship scheme with you… Most importantly, the internet. As part of your job you'll be doing some research online so obviously you'll have unlimited access for that but please <u>don't use it for personal use</u> – **Q15** you'll have your own phones for that.

Some of you have already asked me about flexible working. After your probationary three-month period – some of you will be eligible for this – but <u>it will depend on which department you're in and what your personal circumstances are</u>. So please don't assume you'll automatically be permitted to do this.

*Q16*

I want to make sure there's no confusion about our holiday policy. Apart from any statutory public holidays <u>we ask that you don't book any holidays until after your six-month apprenticeship has finished</u>. Time off should only be taken if you are unwell. Please speak to your supervisor if this is going to be a problem.

*Q17*

You'll be expected to work a 40-hour week but there may be opportunities to do overtime during busy periods. Although you're not required to do this, <u>it can be a valuable experience – so we advise you to take it up if possible</u>. Obviously, we understand that people do have commitments outside work, so don't worry if there are times when you are unavailable.

*Q18*

As you know, we don't have a formal dress code here – you may wear casual clothes as long as they're practical – and the only restriction for shoes we have is on high heels for health and safety reasons. <u>Comfortable shoes like trainers are preferable</u>.

*Q19*

There's a heavily subsidised canteen on site where you can get hot meals or salads cheaply. Snacks and drinks are also provided – so <u>we've decided to introduce a no packed lunch policy</u>. This is partly to encourage healthy eating at work and partly to stop people from eating at their workstation, which is unhygienic.

*Q20*

OK moving on to …

# SECTION 3

| | |
|---|---|
| TUTOR: | OK, so what I'd like you to do now is to talk to your partner about your presentations on urban planning. You should have done most of the reading now, so I'd like you to share your ideas, and talk about the structure of your presentation and what you need to do next. |
| CARLA: | OK Rob. I'm glad we chose quite a specific topic – cities built next to the sea. It made it much easier to find relevant information. |
| ROB: | Yeah. And cities are growing so quickly – I mean, we know that more than half the world's population lives in cities now. |
| CARLA: | Yeah, though that's all cities, not just ones on the coast. But <u>most of the biggest cities are actually built by the sea</u>, I'd not realised that before. |
| ROB: | Nor me. And what's more, a lot of them are built at places where rivers come out into the sea. But apparently this can be a problem. |
| CARLA: | Why? |
| ROB: | Well, as the city expands, agriculture and industry tend to spread further inland along the rivers, and so agriculture moves even further inland up the river. That's not necessarily a problem, except <u>it means more and more pollutants are discharged into the rivers</u>. |
| CARLA: | So these are brought downstream to the cities? |
| ROB: | Right. Hmm. Did you read that article about Miami, on the east coast of the USA? |
| CARLA: | No. |
| ROB: | Well, apparently back in the 1950s they built channels to drain away the water in case of flooding. |
| CARLA: | Sounds sensible. |
| ROB: | Yeah, they spent quite a lot of money on them. <u>But what they didn't take into account was global warming</u>. So they built the drainage channels too close to sea level, and |

Q21

Q22

Q23

now sea levels are rising, they're more or less useless. If there's a lot of rain, the water can't run away, there's nowhere for it to go. The whole design was faulty.

CARLA: So what are the authorities doing about it now?

ROB: I don't know. I did read that they're aiming to stop disposing of waste water into the ocean over the next ten years.

CARLA: But that won't help with flood prevention now, will it?

ROB: No. Really <u>they just need to find the money for something to replace the drainage channels</u>, in order to protect against flooding now. But in the long term they need to consider the whole ecosystem.     *Q24*

CARLA: Right. Really, though, coastal cities can't deal with their problems on their own, can they? I mean, they've got to start acting together at an international level instead of just doing their own thing.

ROB: Absolutely. The thing is, everyone knows what the problems are and environmentalists have a pretty good idea of what we should be doing about them, so <u>they should be able to work together</u> to some extent. But it's going to be a long time before countries come to a decision on what principles they're prepared to abide by.     *Q25*

CARLA: Yes, if they ever do.

--------------------------------------------------------------------------------

CARLA: So I think we've probably got enough for our presentation. It's only fifteen minutes.

ROB: OK. So I suppose we'll begin with some general historical background about why coastal cities were established. But <u>we don't want to spend too long on that</u>, the other students will already know a bit about it. It's all to do with communications and so on.     *Q26*

CARLA: Yes. We should mention some geographical factors, things like wetlands and river estuaries and coastal erosion and so on. We could have some maps of different cities with these features marked.

ROB: On a handout you mean? Or <u>some slides everyone can see</u>?     *Q27*

CARLA: Yeah, that'd be better.

ROB: It'd be good to go into past mistakes in a bit more detail. Did you read that case study of the problems there were in New Orleans with flooding a few years ago?

CARLA: Yes. <u>We could use that as the basis for that part of the talk</u>. I don't think the other students will have read it, but they'll remember hearing about the flooding at the time.     *Q28*

ROB: OK. So that's probably enough background.

CARLA: So then we'll go on to talk about what action's being taken to deal with the problems of coastal cities.

ROB: OK. What else do we need to talk about? Maybe something on future risks, looking more at the long term, if populations continue to grow.

CARLA: Yeah. We'll need to do a bit of work there, I haven't got much information, have you?

ROB: No. <u>We'll need to look at some websites</u>. Shouldn't take too long.     *Q29*

CARLA: OK. And I think we should end by talking about international implications. Maybe <u>we could ask people in the audience</u>. We've got people from quite a lot of different places.     *Q30*

ROB: That'd be interesting, if we have time, yes. So now shall we …

# SECTION 4

Producing enough energy to meet our needs has become a serious problem. Demand is rising rapidly, because of the world's increasing population and expanding <u>industry</u>. Burning fossil fuels, like gas, coal and oil, seriously damages the environment and they'll eventually run out. For a number of years now, scientists have been working out how we can derive energy from     *Q31* renewable sources, such as the sun and wind, without causing pollution. Today I'll outline marine renewable energy – also called ocean energy – which harnesses the movement of the oceans.

Marine renewable energy can be divided into three main categories: wave energy, tidal energy and ocean thermal energy conversion, and I'll say a few words about each one.

First, wave energy. Numerous devices have been invented to harvest wave energy, with names such as Wave Dragon, the Penguin and Mighty Whale, and research is going on to try and come up with a really efficient method. This form of energy has plenty of potential, as the source is <u>constant</u>, and there's no danger of waves coming to a standstill. Electricity can be generated Q32 using onshore systems, using a reservoir, or offshore systems. But the problem with ocean waves is that they're erratic, with the wind making them travel in every <u>direction</u>. This adds to Q33 the difficulty of creating efficient technology: ideally all the waves would travel smoothly and regularly along the same straight line. Another drawback is that sand and other sediment on the ocean <u>floor</u> might be stopped from flowing normally, which can lead to environmental problems. Q34

-------------------------------------------------------------------------------------------------

The second category of marine energy that I'll mention is tidal energy. One major advantage of using the tide, rather than waves, as a source of energy is that it's <u>predictable</u>: we know Q35 the exact times of high and low tides for years to come.

For tidal energy to be effective, the difference between high and low tides needs to be at least five metres, and this occurs naturally in only about forty places on Earth. But the right conditions can be created by constructing a tidal lagoon, an area of sea water separated from the sea.

One current plan is to create a tidal lagoon on the coast of Wales. This will be an area of water within a <u>bay</u> at Swansea, sheltered by a U-shaped breakwater, or dam, built out from the Q36 coast. The breakwater will contain sixteen hydro turbines, and as the tide rises, water rushes through the breakwater, activating the turbines, which turn a generator to produce electricity. Then, for three hours as the tide goes out, the water is held back within the breakwater, increasing the difference in water level, until it's several metres higher within the lagoon than in the open sea. Then, in order to release the stored water, <u>gates</u> in the breakwater are opened. Q37 It pours powerfully out of the lagoon, driving the turbines in the breakwater in the opposite direction and again generating thousands of megawatts of electricity. As there are two high tides a day, this lagoon scheme would generate electricity four times a day, every day, for a total of around 14 hours in every 24 – and enough electricity for over 150,000 homes.

This system has quite a lot in its favour: unlike solar and wind energy it doesn't depend on the weather; the turbines are operated without the need for <u>fuel</u>, so it doesn't create Q38 any greenhouse gas emissions; and very little maintenance is needed. It's estimated that electricity generated in this way will be relatively cheap, and that manufacturing the components would create more than 2,000 <u>jobs</u>, a big boost to the local economy. Q39

On the other hand, there are fears that lagoons might harm both fish and birds, for example by disturbing <u>migration</u> patterns, and causing a build-up of silt, affecting local ecosystems. Q40

There are other forms of tidal energy, but I'll go on to the third category of marine energy: ocean thermal energy conversion. This depends on there being a big difference in temperature between surface water and the water a couple of kilometres below the surface, and this occurs in tropical coastal areas. The idea is to bring cold water up to the surface using a submerged pipe. The concept dates back to 1881, when ...

## TEST 2

## SECTION 1

| | |
|---|---|
| CARL: | Hi, come and take a seat. |
| JULIE: | Thank you. |
| CARL: | My name's Carl Rogers and I'm one of the doctors here at the Total Health Clinic. So I understand this is your first visit to the clinic? |
| JULIE: | Yes, it is. |
| CARL: | OK, well I hope you'll be very happy with the service you receive here. So if it's alright with you I'll take a few details to help me give you the best possible service. |
| JULIE: | Sure. |
| CARL: | So can I check first of all that we have the correct personal details for you? So your full name is Julie Anne <u>Garcia</u>? |
| JULIE: | That's correct. |
| CARL: | Perfect. And can I have a contact phone number? |
| JULIE: | It's <u>219 442 9785</u>. |
| CARL: | OK, and then can I just check that we have the correct date of birth? |
| JULIE: | <u>October tenth</u>, 1992. |
| CARL: | Oh, I actually have 1991, I'll just correct that now. Right, so that's all good. Now I just need just a few more personal details ... do you have an occupation, either full-time or part-time? |
| JULIE: | Yes, I work full-time in Esterhazy's – you know, the restaurant chain. I started off as a waitress there a few years ago and I'm a <u>manager</u> now. |
| CARL: | Oh I know them, yeah, they're down on 114th Street, aren't they? |
| JULIE: | That's right. |
| CARL: | Yeah, I've been there a few times. I just love their salads. |
| JULIE: | That's good to hear. |
| CARL: | Right, so one more thing I need to know before we talk about why you're here, Julie, and that's the name of your insurance company. |
| JULIE: | It's <u>Cawley</u> Life Insurance, that's C-A-W-L-E-Y. |
| CARL: | Excellent, thank you so much. |

The "Example", "Q1"–"Q4" markers appear in the right margin alongside the dialogue above (Example = Garcia; Q1 = 219 442 9785; Q2 = October tenth; Q3 = manager; Q4 = Cawley).

----------------------------------------------------------------

| | |
|---|---|
| CARL: | Now Julie, let's look at how we can help you. So tell me a little about what brought you here today. |
| JULIE: | Well, I've been getting a pain in my <u>knee</u>, the left one. Not very serious at first, but it's gotten worse, so I thought I ought to see someone about it. |
| CARL: | That's certainly the right decision. So how long have you been aware of this pain? Is it just a few days, or is it longer than that? |
| JULIE: | Longer. It's been worse for the last couple of days, but it's <u>three weeks</u> since I first noticed it. It came on quite gradually though, so I kind of ignored it at first. |
| CARL: | And have you taken any medication yourself, or treated it in anyway? |
| JULIE: | Yeah, I've been taking medication to deal with the pain, Tylenol, and that works OK for a few hours. But I don't like to keep taking it. |
| CARL: | OK. And what about heat treatment? Have you tried applying heat at all? |
| JULIE: | No, but I have been using ice on it for the last few days. |
| CARL: | And does that seem to help the pain at all? |
| JULIE: | A little, yes. |
| CARL: | Good. Now you look as if you're quite fit normally? |

The "Q5" and "Q6" markers appear in the right margin (Q5 = knee; Q6 = three weeks).

| JULIE: | I am, yes. | |
|---|---|---|
| CARL: | So do you do any sport on a regular basis? | |
| JULIE: | Yes, I play a lot of <u>tennis</u>. I belong to a club so I go there a lot. I'm quite competitive so I enjoy that side of it as well as the exercise. But I haven't gone since this started. | Q7 |
| CARL: | Sure. And do you do any other types of exercise? | |
| JULIE: | Yeah, I sometimes do a little swimming, but usually just when I'm on vacation. But normally I go <u>running</u> a few times a week, maybe three or four times. | Q8 |
| CARL: | Hmm. So your legs are getting quite a pounding. But you haven't had any problems up to now? | |
| JULIE: | No, not with my legs. I did have an accident last year when I slipped and hurt my <u>shoulder</u>, but that's better now. | Q9 |
| CARL: | Excellent. And do you have any allergies? | |
| JULIE: | No, none that I'm aware of. | |
| CARL: | And do you take any medication on a regular basis? | |
| JULIE: | Well, I take <u>vitamins</u> but that's all. I'm generally very healthy. | Q10 |
| CARL: | OK, well let's have a closer look and see what might be causing this problem. If you can just get up … | |

# SECTION 2

We'll be arriving at Branley Castle in about five minutes, but before we get there I'll give you a little information about the castle and what our visit will include.

So in fact there's been a castle on this site for over eleven hundred years. The first building was a fort constructed in 914 AD for defence against Danish invaders by King Alfred the Great's daughter, who ruled England at the time. In the following century, after the Normans conquered England, the land was given to a nobleman called Richard de Vere, and he built a castle there that stayed in the de Vere family for over four hundred years.

However, when Queen Elizabeth I announced that she was going to visit the castle in 1576 it was beginning to look a bit run down, and it was decided that rather than repair the guest rooms, <u>they'd make a new house for her</u> out of wood next to the main hall. She stayed there    Q11
for four nights and apparently it was very luxurious, but unfortunately it was destroyed a few years later by fire.

In the seventeenth century the castle belonged to the wealthy Fenys family, who enlarged it and made it more comfortable. However, by 1982 the Fenys family could no longer afford to maintain the castle, even though they received government support, and they put it on the market. It was eventually taken over by <u>a company who owned a number of amusement</u>    Q12
<u>parks</u>, but when we get there I think you'll see that they've managed to retain the original atmosphere of the castle.

When you go inside, you'll find that in the state rooms <u>there are life-like moving wax models</u>    Q13
<u>dressed in costumes of different periods in the past</u>, which even carry on conversations together. As well as that, in every room there are booklets giving information about what the room was used for and the history of the objects and furniture it contains.

The castle park's quite extensive. At one time sheep were kept there, and in the nineteenth century the owners had a little zoo with animals like rabbits and even a baby elephant. Nowadays the old zoo buildings are used for <u>public displays of paintings and sculpture</u>. The park also has some beautiful trees, though the oldest of all, which dated back 800 years, was sadly blown down in 1987.

*Q14*

Now, you're free to wander around on your own until 4.30, but then at the end of our visit we'll all meet together at the bottom of the Great Staircase. We'll then go on to the long gallery, where there's a wonderful collection of photographs showing the family who owned the castle a hundred years ago having tea and cakes in the conservatory – and we'll then take you to <u>the same place, where afternoon tea will be served</u> to you.

*Q15*

-------------------------------------------------------------------------------

Now if you can take a look at your plans you'll see Branley Castle has four towers, joined together by a high wall, with the river on two sides.

Don't miss seeing the Great Hall. That's near the river in the main tower, the biggest one, which was extended and redesigned in the eighteenth century.

If you want to get a good view of the whole castle, you can walk around the walls. <u>The starting point's quite near the main entrance – walk straight down the path until you get to the south gate, and it's just there.</u> Don't go on to the north gate – there's no way up from there.

*Q16*

There'll shortly be a show in which you can see archers displaying their skill with a bow and arrow. The quickest way to get there is to <u>take the first left after the main entrance and follow the path past the bridge, then you'll see it in front of you at the end.</u>

*Q17*

If you like animals there's also a display of hunting birds – falcons and eagles and so on. If you <u>go from the main entrance in the direction of the south gate, but turn right before you get there instead of going through it, you'll see it on your right past the first tower.</u>

*Q18*

At 3 pm there's a short performance of traditional dancing on the <u>outdoor stage. That's right at the other side of the castle from the entrance, and over the bridge</u>. It's about ten minutes' walk or so.

*Q19*

And finally the shop. It's actually <u>inside one of the towers, but the way in is from the outside. Just take the first left after the main entrance, go down the path and take the first right</u>. It's got some lovely gifts and souvenirs.

*Q20*

Right, so we're just arriving …

# SECTION 3

| | |
|---|---|
| TUTOR: | So, Rosie and Martin, let's look at what you've got for your presentation on woolly mammoths. |
| ROSIE: | OK, we've got a short outline here. |
| TUTOR: | Thanks. So it's about a research project in North America? |
| MARTIN: | Yes. But we thought we needed something general about woolly mammoths in our introduction, to establish that they were related to our modern elephant, and they lived thousands of years ago in the last ice age. |
| ROSIE: | Maybe we could show a video clip of a cartoon about mammoths. But that'd be a bit childish. Or we could have a diagram, <u>it could be a timeline to show when they lived, with illustrations</u>?  *Q21* |
| MARTIN: | Or we could just show a drawing of them walking in the ice? No, let's go with your last suggestion. |
| TUTOR: | Good. Then you're describing the discovery of the mammoth tooth on St Paul's Island in Alaska, and why it was significant. |
| ROSIE: | Yes. The tooth was found by a man called Russell Graham. He picked it up from under a rock in a cave. He knew it was special – for a start it was in really good condition, as if it had been just extracted from the animal's jawbone. Anyway, they found it was 6,500 years old. |
| TUTOR: | So why was that significant? |
| ROSIE: | Well <u>the mammoth bones previously found on the North American mainland were much less recent than that</u>. So this was really amazing.  *Q22* |
| MARTIN: | Then we're making an animated diagram to show the geography of the area in prehistoric times. So originally, St Paul's Island wasn't an island, it was connected to the mainland, and mammoths and other animals like bears were able to roam around the whole area. |
| ROSIE: | Then the climate warmed up and the sea level began to rise, and the island got cut off from the mainland. So <u>those mammoths on the island couldn't escape; they had to stay on the island</u>.  *Q23* |
| MARTIN: | And in fact the species survived there for thousands of years after they'd become extinct on the mainland. |
| TUTOR: | So why do you think they died out on the mainland? |
| ROSIE: | No one's sure. |
| MARTIN: | Anyway, next we'll explain how Graham and his team identified the date when the mammoths became extinct on the *island*. They concluded that <u>the extinction happened 5,600 years ago, which is a very precise time for a prehistoric extinction</u>. It's based on samples they took from mud at the bottom of a lake on the island. They analysed it to find out what had fallen in over time – bits of plants, volcanic ash and even DNA from the mammoths themselves. It's standard procedure, but it took nearly two years to do.  *Q24* |

----

| | |
|---|---|
| TUTOR: | So why don't you quickly go through the main sections of your presentation and discuss what action's needed for each part? |
| MARTIN: | OK. So for the introduction, we're using a visual, so once we've prepared that we're done. |
| ROSIE: | I'm not sure. I think <u>we need to write down all the ideas we want to include here</u>, not just rely on memory. How we begin the presentation is so important …  *Q25* |
| MARTIN: | You're right. |
| ROSIE: | The discovery of the mammoth tooth is probably the most dramatic part, but we don't have that much information, only what we got from the online article. I thought maybe <u>we could get in touch with the researcher who led the team and ask him to tell us a bit more</u>.  *Q26* |

| | |
|---|---|
| MARTIN: | Great idea. What about the section with the initial questions asked by the researchers? We've got a lot on that but we need to make it interesting. |
| ROSIE: | We could <u>ask the audience to suggest some questions about it and then see how</u> <u>many of them we can answer</u>. I don't think it would take too long.      Q27 |
| TUTOR: | Yes that would add a bit of variety. |
| MARTIN: | Then the section on further research carried out on the island – analysing the mud in the lake. I wonder if we've actually got too much information here, should we cut some? |
| ROSIE: | I don't think so, but it's all a bit muddled at present. |
| MARTIN: | Yes, <u>maybe it would be better if it followed a chronological pattern</u>.      Q28 |
| ROSIE: | I think so. The findings and possible explanations section is just about ready, but we need to practise it <u>so we're sure it won't overrun</u>.      Q29 |
| MARTIN: | I think it should be OK, but yes, let's make sure. |
| TUTOR: | In the last section, relevance to the present day, you've got some good ideas but this is where you need to move away from the ideas of others and <u>give your own</u> <u>viewpoint</u>.      Q30 |
| MARTIN: | OK, we'll think about that. Now shall we … |

# SECTION 4

In this series of lectures about the history of weather forecasting, I'll start by examining its early history – that'll be the subject of today's talk.

OK, so we'll start by going back thousands of years. Most ancient cultures had weather gods, and weather catastrophes, such as floods, played an important role in many creation myths. Generally, weather was attributed to the whims of the gods, as the wide range of weather gods in various cultures shows. For instance, there's the Egyptian sun god Ra, and Thor, the Norse god of thunder and lightning. Many ancient civilisations developed rites such as <u>dances</u> in order to make the weather gods look kindly on them.      Q31

But the weather was of daily importance: observing the skies and drawing the correct conclusions from these observations was really important, in fact their <u>survival</u> depended on   Q32 it. It isn't known when people first started to observe the skies, but at around 650 BC, the Babylonians produced the first short-range weather forecasts, based on their observations of <u>clouds</u> and other phenomena. The Chinese also recognised weather patterns, and by   Q33 300 BC, astronomers had developed a calendar which divided the year into 24 <u>festivals</u>, each   Q34 associated with a different weather phenomenon.

The ancient Greeks were the first to develop a more scientific approach to explaining the weather. The work of the philosopher and scientist Aristotle, in the fourth century BC, is especially noteworthy, as his ideas held sway for nearly 2,000 years. In 340 BC, he wrote a book in which he attempted to account for the formation of rain, clouds, wind and storms. He also described celestial phenomena such as haloes – that is, bright circles of light around the sun, the moon and bright stars – and <u>comets</u>. Many of his observations were surprisingly   Q35 accurate. For example, he believed that heat could cause water to evaporate. But he also jumped to quite a few wrong conclusions, such as that winds are breathed out by the Earth. Errors like this were rectified from the Renaissance onwards.

-----

For nearly 2,000 years, Aristotle's work was accepted as the chief authority on weather theory. Alongside this, though, in the Middle Ages weather observations were passed on in the form of proverbs, such as 'Red <u>sky</u> at night, shepherd's delight; red sky in the morning, shepherd's warning'. Many of these are based on very good observations and are accurate, as contemporary meteorologists have discovered.

*Q36*

For centuries, any attempt to forecast the weather could only be based on personal observations, but in the fifteenth century scientists began to see the need for <u>instruments</u>. Until then, the only ones available were weather vanes – to determine the wind direction – and early versions of rain gauges. One of the first, invented in the fifteenth century, was a hygrometer, which measured humidity. This was one of many inventions that contributed to the development of weather forecasting.

*Q37*

In 1592, the Italian scientist and inventor Galileo developed the world's first <u>thermometer</u>. His student Torricelli later invented the barometer, which allowed people to measure atmospheric pressure. In 1648, the French philosopher Pascal proved that pressure decreases with altitude. This discovery was verified by English astronomer Halley in 1686; and Halley was also the first person to map trade winds.

*Q38*

This increasing ability to measure factors related to weather helped scientists to understand the atmosphere and its processes better, and they started collecting weather observation data systematically. In the eighteenth century, the scientist and politician Benjamin Franklin carried out work on electricity and lightning in particular, but he was also very interested in weather and studied it throughout most of his life. It was Franklin who discovered that <u>storms</u> generally travel from west to east.

*Q39*

In addition to new meteorological instruments, other developments contributed to our understanding of the atmosphere. People in different locations began to keep records, and in the mid-nineteenth century, the invention of the <u>telegraph</u> made it possible for these records to be collated. This led, by the end of the nineteenth century, to the first weather services.

*Q40*

It was not until the early twentieth century that mathematics and physics became part of meteorology, and we'll continue from that point next week.

## TEST 3

## SECTION 1

| | |
|---|---|
| ANGELA: | Hello, Flanders conference hotel. |
| MAN: | Oh, hi. I wanted to ask about conference facilities at the hotel. Have I come through to the right person? |
| ANGELA: | You have. I'm the customer services manager. My name's <u>Angela</u>. So how can I help you? |
| MAN: | Well, I'm calling from Barrett and Stansons, we're a medical company based in Perth. |
| ANGELA: | Oh yes. |
| MAN: | And we're organising a conference for our clients to be held in Sydney. It'll be held over two days and we're expecting about fifty or sixty people. |
| ANGELA: | When were you thinking of having it? |
| MAN: | Some time early next year, like the end of January? It'd have to be a weekend. |
| ANGELA: | Let me see … our conference facilities are already booked for the weekend beginning January 28th. We could do the first weekend in February? |
| MAN: | How about January 21st? |
| ANGELA: | I'm afraid that's booked too. |
| MAN: | Well, let's go for the February date then. |
| ANGELA: | So that's the weekend beginning the 4th. |
| MAN: | OK. Now can you tell me a bit about what conference facilities you have? |
| ANGELA: | Sure. So for talks and presentations we have the Tesla room. |
| MAN: | Sorry? |
| ANGELA: | <u>Tesla</u> – that's spelled T-E-S-L-A. It holds up to a hundred people, and it's fully equipped with a projector and so on. |
| MAN: | How about a <u>microphone</u>? |
| ANGELA: | Yes, that'll be all set up ready for you, and there'll be one that members of the audience can use too, for questions, if necessary. |
| MAN: | Fine. And we'll also need some sort of open area where people can sit and have a cup of coffee, and we'd like to have an <u>exhibition</u> of our products and services there as well, so that'll need to be quite a big space. |
| ANGELA: | That's fine, there's a central atrium with all those facilities, and you can come before the conference starts if you want to set everything up. |
| MAN: | Great. And I presume there's <u>wifi</u>? |
| ANGELA: | Oh yes, that's free and available throughout the hotel. |
| MAN: | OK. |
| ANGELA: | Would you also like us to provide a buffet lunch? We can do a two-course meal with a number of different options. |
| MAN: | What sort of price are we looking at for that? |
| ANGELA: | Well, I can send you a copy of the standard menu. That's $<u>45</u> per person. Or you can have the special for $25 more. |
| MAN: | I think the standard should be OK, but yes, send me the menu. |

Q1
Q2
Q3
Q4
Q5

---

| | |
|---|---|
| MAN: | Now we're also going to need accommodation on the Saturday night for some of the participants … I'm not sure how many, but probably about 25. So what do you charge for a room? |
| ANGELA: | Well, for conference attendees we have a 25% reduction, so we can offer you rooms at $<u>135</u>. Normally a standard room's $180. |

Q6

| | |
|---|---|
| MAN: | And does that include breakfast? |
| ANGELA: | Sure. And of course, guests can also make use of all the other facilities at the hotel. So we've got a spa where you can get massages and facials and so on, and there's a <u>pool</u> up on the roof for the use of guests. |
| MAN: | Great. Now what about transport links? The hotel's downtown, isn't it? |
| ANGELA: | Yes, it's about 12 kilometres from the <u>airport</u>, but there's a complimentary shuttle bus for guests. And it's only about ten minutes' walk from the central railway station. |
| MAN: | OK. Now, I don't know Sydney very well, can you just give me an idea of the location of the hotel? |
| ANGELA: | Well, it's downtown on Wilby Street, that's quite a small street, and it's not very far from the <u>sea</u>. And of course if the conference attendees want to go out on the Saturday evening there's a huge choice of places to eat. Then if they want to make a night of it, they can go on to one of the <u>clubs</u> in the area – there are a great many to choose from. |
| MAN: | OK. So if we go ahead with this, can you give me some information about how much … |

*Q7* (aligned with pool line)
*Q8* (aligned with airport line)
*Q9* (aligned with sea line)
*Q10* (aligned with clubs line)

## SECTION 2

Good morning. My name's Lucy Crittenden, and I'm the Director of Operations for an organisation that arranges volunteering in this part of the country. I'm hoping I can persuade one or two of you to become volunteers yourselves. Let me start by briefly explaining what we mean by volunteering.

Volunteers are teenagers and adults who choose to spend some time, unpaid, helping other people in some way. Most volunteers devote two or three hours to this every week, while a few do much more. The people they help may have physical or behavioural difficulties, for example.

Volunteers can do all sorts of things, depending on their own abilities and interests. If they're supporting a family that's struggling, for example, they may be able to give them tips on cooking, or recommend how to plan their budget or how to shop sensibly on their income. They might even do <u>some painting or wallpapering</u>, perhaps alongside any members of the [Q11] family who are able to do it. Or even do <u>some babysitting</u> so that parents can go out for [Q12] a while.

The benefit from volunteering isn't only for the people being helped. Volunteers also gain from it: they're using their skills to cope with somebody's mental or physical ill health, and <u>volunteering may be a valuable element of their CV when they're applying for jobs</u>: employers [Q13] usually look favourably on someone who's given up time to help others. Significantly, most volunteers <u>feel that what they're doing gives them a purpose in their lives</u>. And in my opinion, [Q14] they're lucky in that respect, as many people don't have that feeling.

----

Now I'd like to tell you what some of our volunteers have said about what they do, to give you an idea of the range of ways in which they can help people.

Habib supports an elderly lady who's beginning to show signs of dementia. Once a week they, along with other elderly people, go to the local community centre, where a group of people come in and sing. The songs <u>take the listeners back to their youth</u>, and for a little [Q15] while they can forget the difficulties that they face now.

Our volunteer Consuela is an amazing woman. <u>She has difficulty walking herself, but she doesn't let that stop her.</u> She helps a couple of people with similar difficulties, who had almost stopped walking altogether. <u>By using herself as an example, Consuela encourages them to walk more and more.</u>   Q16

Minh visits a young man who lives alone and can't leave his home on his own, so he hardly ever saw anyone. But together <u>they go out to the cinema, or to see friends</u> the young man   Q17
hadn't been able to visit for a long time.

Tanya visits an elderly woman once a week. When the woman found out that Tanya is a professional dressmaker, she got interested. Tanya showed her some soft toys she'd made, and <u>the woman decided to try it herself</u>. And now she really enjoys it, and spends hours   Q18
making toys. They're not perhaps up to Tanya's standard yet, but she gains a lot of pleasure from doing it.

Alexei is a volunteer with a family that faces a number of difficulties. By calmly talking over possible solutions with family members, he's helping them to realise that they aren't helpless, and that <u>they can do something themselves to improve their situation</u>. This has been great for   Q19
their self-esteem.

And the last volunteer I'll mention, though there are plenty more, is Juba. She volunteers with a teenage girl with learning difficulties, who wasn't very good at talking to other people. Juba's worked very patiently with her, <u>and now the girl is far better at expressing herself, and</u>   Q20
<u>at understanding other people.</u>

OK, I hope that's given you an idea of what volunteering is all about. Now I'd like …

## SECTION 3

| | |
|---|---|
| LIZZIE: | So how are you getting on with your teaching practice at the High School, Joe? |
| JOE: | Well I've been put in charge of the school marching band, and it's quite a responsibility. I'd like to talk it over with you. |
| LIZZIE: | Go ahead. You'd better start by giving me a bit of background. |
| JOE: | OK. Well the band has students in it from all years, so they're aged 11 to 18, and there are about <u>50</u> of them altogether. It's quite a popular activity within the school. I've never worked with a band of more than 20 before, and this is very different. |

Q21

| | |
|---|---|
| LIZZIE: | I can imagine. |
| JOE: | They aren't really good enough to enter national band competitions, but they're in a <u>regional</u> one later in the term. Even if they don't win, and I don't expect them to, hopefully it'll be an incentive for them to try and improve. |

Q22

| | |
|---|---|
| LIZZIE: | Yes, hopefully. |
| JOE: | Well, now the town council's organising a <u>carnival</u> in the summer, and the band has been asked to perform. If you ask me, they aren't really up to it yet, and I need to get them functioning better as a band, and in a very short time. |

Q23

| | |
|---|---|
| LIZZIE: | Have you been doing anything with them? Apart from practising the music, I mean. |
| JOE: | I played a recording I came across, of a <u>drummer</u> talking about how playing in a band had changed his life. I think it was an after-dinner speech. I thought it was pretty inspiring, because being in the band had stopped him from getting involved in crime. The students seemed to find it interesting, too. |

Q24

| LIZZIE: | That's good. | |
|---|---|---|
| JOE: | I'm planning to show them that old <u>film</u> from the 1940s 'Strike Up the Band', and talk about it with the students. What do you think? | Q25 |
| LIZZIE: | Good idea. As it's about a school band, it might make the students realise how much they can achieve if they work together. | |
| JOE: | That's what I've got in mind. I'm hoping I can take some of the band to a <u>parade</u> that's going to take place next month. A couple of marching bands will be performing, and the atmosphere should be quite exciting. It depends on whether I can persuade the school to hire a coach or two to take us there. | Q26 |
| LIZZIE: | Mmm. They sound like good ideas to me. | |
| JOE: | Thanks. | |

--------------------------------------------------------------------------------

| JOE: | Can I tell you about a few people in the band who I'm finding it quite difficult to cope with? I'm sure you'll have some ideas about what I can do. | |
|---|---|---|
| LIZZIE: | Go ahead. | |
| JOE: | There's a flautist who says she loves playing in the band. We rehearse twice a week after school, but <u>she's hardly ever there</u>. Then she looks for me the next day and gives me a very plausible reason – she says she had to help her mother, or she's been ill, but to be honest, I don't believe her. | Q27 |
| LIZZIE: | Oh dear! Any more students with difficulties? | |
| JOE: | Plenty! There's a trumpeter who thinks she's the best musician in the band, though she certainly isn't. <u>She's always saying what she thinks other people should do</u>, which makes my job pretty difficult. | Q28 |
| LIZZIE: | She sounds a bit of a nightmare! | |
| JOE: | You can say that again. One of the trombonists has got an impressive sense of rhythm, and could be an excellent musician – except that <u>he has breathing difficulties, and he doesn't really have enough breath for the trombone</u>. He'd be much better off playing percussion, for instance, but he refuses to give up. So he ends up only playing half the notes. | Q29 |
| LIZZIE: | I suppose you have to admire his determination. | |
| JOE: | Maybe. One of the percussionists isn't too bad, but <u>he never seems to interact with other people, and he always rushes off as soon as the rehearsal ends</u>. I don't know if there are family reasons, or what. But it isn't good in a band, where people really need to feel they're part of a group. | Q30 |
| LIZZIE: | Hmm. | |
| JOE: | There are others too, but at least that gives you an idea of what I'm up against. Do you have any thoughts about what I can do, Lizzie? | |

# SECTION 4

As you all know, the university is planning an arts festival for later this year, and here in the music department we've planned three concerts. These will be public performances, and the programme has just been finalised. The theme of the festival is links between the UK and Australia, and this is reflected in the music: each concert will feature both British and Australian composers. I'll tell you briefly about the Australian music, as you probably won't be familiar with that.

The first concert will include music by Liza Lim, who was born in Perth, Western Australia, in 1966. As a child, Lim originally learned to play the piano – like so many children – and also the <u>violin</u>, but when she was 11 her teachers encouraged her to start composing. She found    *Q31* this was her real strength, and she studied and later taught composition, both in Australia and in other countries. As a composer, she has received commissions from numerous orchestras, other performers and festivals in several countries.

Liza Lim's compositions are vibrant and full of <u>energy</u>, and she often explores Asian and    *Q32* Australian Aboriginal cultural sources, including the native instrument, the didgeridoo: this is featured in a work called *The Compass.* Her music is very expressive, so although it is <u>complex</u>, it has the power of connecting with audiences and performers alike.    *Q33*

In the festival we're going to give a semi-staged performance of *The Oresteia*. This is an <u>opera</u> in seven parts, based on the trilogy of ancient Greek tragedies by Aeschylus. Lim    *Q34* composed this when she was in her mid-20s, and she also wrote the text, along with Barrie Kosky. It's performed by six singers, a dancer, and an orchestra that, as well as standard orchestral instruments, includes electric guitar, and a traditional Turkish stringed instrument. Lim wrote that because the stories in the tragedies are not easy to tell, the sounds she creates are also <u>disturbing</u>, and they include breathing, sobbing, laughing and whistling. The    *Q35* work lasts around 75 minutes, and the rest of the concert will consist of orchestral works by the British composers Ralph Vaughan Williams and Frederick Delius.

-----------------------------------------------------------------------------------------------------------------

Moving on now to our second concert, this will begin with instrumental music by British composers – Benjamin Britten and Judith Weir. After the interval we'll go to Australia for a piece by Ross Edwards: *The Tower of Remoteness.* According to Edwards, the inspiration for this piece came from nature, when he was sitting alone in the dry bed of a creek, overshadowed by the leaves of palm trees, listening to the birds and insects. *The Tower of Remoteness* is scored for piano and <u>clarinet</u>. Edwards says he realised years after writing the    *Q36* piece that he had subconsciously modelled its opening phrase on a bird call.

Ross Edwards was born in 1943 in Sydney, Australia, and studied at the Sydney Conservatorium of Music and the universities of Adelaide and Sydney. He's well known in Australia, and in fact he's one of the country's most performed composers. He's written a wide range of music, from symphonies and concertos to some composed specifically for children. Edwards's music has been described as being 'deeply connected to Australia', and it can be regarded as a celebration of the <u>diversity</u> of cultures that Australia can be proud of.    *Q37*

The last of the three Australian composers to be represented in our festival is Carl Vine. Born in 1954, Vine, like Liza Lim, comes from Perth, Western Australia. He took up the cornet at the age of five, switching to the piano five years later. However, he went to university to study <u>physics</u>, before changing to composition. After graduating he moved to Sydney and worked    *Q38* as a freelance pianist and composer. Before long he had become prominent in Australia as a composer for <u>dance</u>, and in fact has written 25 scores of that type.    *Q39*

In our third concert, Vine will be represented by his music for the flag hand-over ceremony of the <u>Olympics</u> held in 1996. This seven-minute orchestral piece was of course heard by    *Q40* millions of people worldwide, and we'll hear it alongside works written by British composers Edward Elgar and, more recently, Thomas Adès.

# TEST 4

## SECTION 1

| | |
|---|---|
| ANDREW: | Good morning, Clare House Hotel. Andrew speaking. I'm the <u>Events</u> Manager. |
| SAM: | Good morning, Andrew. My name's Samantha. I'm arranging a party for my parents' fiftieth wedding anniversary, and I'm ringing to ask about hiring a room some time next September. Also my parents and several of the guests will need accommodation. |
| ANDREW: | OK, I'm sure we can help you with that. Will you be having a sit-down meal or a buffet? |
| SAM: | Probably a sit-down. |
| ANDREW: | And do you know how many people there'll be? |
| SAM: | Around eighty, I think. |
| ANDREW: | Well we have two rooms that can hold that number. One is the Adelphi Room. That can seat <u>eighty-five</u>, or hold over a hundred if people are standing for a buffet. |
| SAM: | Right. |
| ANDREW: | If you have live music, there's room for four or five musicians in the gallery overlooking the room. Our guests usually appreciate the fact that the music can be loud enough for dancing, but not too loud for conversation. |
| SAM: | Yes, I really don't like it when you can't talk. |
| ANDREW: | Exactly. Now the Adelphi Room is at the back of the hotel, and there are French windows leading out onto the terrace. This has a beautiful display of pots of <u>roses</u> at that time of the year. |
| SAM: | Which direction does it face? |
| ANDREW: | Southwest, so that side of the hotel gets the sun in the afternoon and early evening. |
| SAM: | Very nice. |
| ANDREW: | From the terrace you can see the area of <u>trees</u> within the grounds of the hotel, or you can stroll through there to the river – that's on the far side, so it isn't visible from the hotel. |
| SAM: | OK. |
| ANDREW: | Then another option is the Carlton Room. This is a bit bigger – it can hold up to a hundred and ten people – and it has the advantage of a <u>stage</u>, which is useful if you have any entertainment, or indeed a small band can fit onto it. |
| SAM: | And can you go outside from the room? |
| ANDREW: | No, the Carlton Room is on the first floor, but on one side the windows look out onto the lake. |
| SAM: | Lovely. I think either of those rooms would be suitable. |
| ANDREW: | Can I tell you about some of the options we offer in addition? |
| SAM: | Please do. |
| ANDREW: | As well as a meal, you can have an MC, a Master of Ceremonies, who'll be with you throughout the party. |
| SAM: | What exactly is the MC's function? I suppose they make a <u>speech</u> during the meal if we need one, do they? |
| ANDREW: | That's right. All our MCs are trained as public speakers, so they can easily get people's attention – many guests are glad to have someone who can make themselves heard above the chatter! And they're also your <u>support</u> – if anything goes wrong, the MC will deal with it, so you can relax. |

*Example*

Q1

Q2

Q3

Q4

Q5

Q6

| SAM: | Great! I'll need to ask you about food, but something else that's important is accommodation. You obviously have rooms in the hotel, but do you also have any other accommodation, like <u>cabins</u>, for example? | Q7 |
| ANDREW: | Yes, there are five in the grounds, all self-contained. They each sleep two to four people and have their own living room, bathroom and small kitchen. | |
| SAM: | That sounds perfect for what we'll need. | |

-------------------------------------------------------------------------------------------------------------

| SAM: | Now you have various facilities, don't you? Are they all included in the price of hiring the room? The pool, for instance. | |
| ANDREW: | Normally you'd be able to use it, but <u>it'll be closed throughout September for refurbishment</u>, I'm afraid. <u>The gym will be available, though, at no extra charge.</u> That's open all day, from six in the morning until midnight. | Q8 Q9 |
| SAM: | Right. | |
| ANDREW: | And the tennis courts, but <u>there is a small additional payment for those</u>. We have four courts, and it's worth booking in advance if you possibly can, as there can be quite a long waiting list for them! | Q10 |
| SAM: | Right. Now could we discuss the food? This would be dinner, around seven o'clock ... | |

# SECTION 2

Hello everyone. I'm Jake Stevens and I'm your rep here at the hotel. I'm sure you'll all have a great time here. So let me tell you a bit about what's on offer. I'll start by telling you about some of the excursions that are available for guests.

One thing you have to do while you're here is go dolphin watching. On our boat trips, we pretty well guarantee you'll see dolphins – if you don't you can repeat the trip free of charge. We organise daily trips for just 35 euros. Unfortunately <u>there aren't any places left for this</u> Q11 <u>afternoon's trip</u>, but come and see me to book for later in the week.

If you're energetic, I'd recommend our forest walk. It's a guided walk of about seven kilometres. There'll be a stop half way, and <u>you'll be provided with a drink and sandwiches</u>. Q12 There's some fairly steep climbs up the hills, so you need to be reasonably fit for this one, with good shoes, and bring a waterproof in case it rains. It's just 25 euros all inclusive, and it's every Wednesday.

Then on Thursdays we organise a cycle trip, which will give you all the fun of biking without the effort. We'll take you and your bike up to the top of Mount Larna, and leave you to bike back – <u>it's a 700-metre drop in just 20 kilometres</u> so this isn't really for inexperienced cyclists Q13 as you'll be going pretty fast. And if it's a clear day, you'll have fantastic views.

On our local craft tour you can find out about the traditional activities in the island. And the best thing about this trip is that <u>it's completely free</u>. You'll be taken to a factory where Q14 jewellery is made, and also a ceramics centre. If you want, you can buy some of the products but that's entirely up to you. The trip starts after lunch on Thursday, and you'll return by 6 pm.

If you're interested in astronomy you may already know that the island's one of the best places in the world to observe the night sky. We can offer trips to the observatory on Friday for those who are interested. They cost 90 euros per person and you'll be shown the huge telescopes and have a talk from an expert, who'll explain all about how they work. <u>Afterwards</u> Q15 <u>we'll head down to Sunset Beach, where you can have a dip in the ocean</u> if you want before we head off back to the hotel.

Finally, there's horse riding. This is organised by the Equestrian Centre over near Playa Cortino and it's a great experience if you're a keen horseback rider, <u>or even if you've never been on a horse before</u>. They take you down to the beach, and you can canter along the sand and through the waves. It costs 35 euros and it's available every day.

*Q16*

---

So there's plenty to do in the daytime, but what about night life?

Well, the number one attraction's called 'Musical Favourites'. Guests enjoy a three-course meal and unlimited free drinks, and watch a fantastic show, starting with musicals set in Paris and then crossing the Atlantic to Las Vegas and finally Copacabana. At the end the <u>cast members come down from the stage</u>, still in their stunning costumes, and <u>you'll have a chance to chat with them</u>. It's hugely popular, so let me know now if you're interested because <u>it's no good leaving it until the last minute</u>. It's on Friday night. Tickets are just 50 euros each, but for an extra 10 euros you can have a table right by the stage.

*Q17*
*Q18*

If you'd like to go back in time, there's the *Castle Feast* on Saturday evening. It's held in a twelfth-century castle, and you eat in the great courtyard, with ladies in long gowns serving your food. You're given a whole chicken each, which you eat in the medieval way, <u>using your hands instead of cutlery</u>, and you're entertained by competitions where the horseback riders attempt to knock one another off their horses. Then you can watch the dancers in the ballroom and <u>join in as well if you want</u>. OK, so now if anyone ...

*Q19*
*Q20*

## SECTION 3

| | |
|---|---|
| STEPHANIE: | Hello, Trevor. |
| TREVOR: | Hello, Stephanie. You said you wanted to talk about the course I'm taking on literature for children. |
| STEPHANIE: | That's right. I'm thinking of doing it next year, but I'd like to find out more about it first. |
| TREVOR: | OK, well, as you probably know, it's a one-year course. It's divided into six modules, and you have to take all of them. One of the most interesting ones, for me, at least, was about the purpose of children's literature. |
| STEPHANIE: | You mean, whether it should just entertain children or should be educational, as well. |
| TREVOR: | Right, and whether the teaching should be factual – giving them information about the world – or ethical, teaching them values. What's fascinating is that <u>the writer isn't necessarily conscious of the message they're conveying</u>. For instance, a story might show a child who has a problem as a result of not doing what an adult has told them to do, implying that children should always obey adults. |
| STEPHANIE: | I see what you mean. |
| TREVOR: | That module made me realise how important stories are – they can have a significant effect on children as they grow up. Actually, <u>it inspired me to have a go at it myself</u>, just for my own interest. I know I can't compete with the really popular stories, like the Harry Potter books – they're very good, and even young kids like my seven-year-old niece love reading them. |
| STEPHANIE: | Mm. I'm very interested in illustrations in stories. Is that covered in the course? |
| TREVOR: | Yes, there's a module on pictures, and how they're sometimes central to the story. |

*Q21*
*Q22*

| | |
|---|---|
| STEPHANIE: | That's good. I remember some frightening ones I saw as a child and I can still see them vividly in my mind, years later! Pictures can be so powerful, just as powerful as words. I've always enjoyed drawing, so <u>that's the field I want to go into when I finish the course</u>. I bet that module will be really helpful. |
| TREVOR: | I'm sure it will. We also studied comics in that module, but I'm not convinced of their value, not compared with books. One of the great things about words is that you use your imagination, but with a comic you don't have to. |
| STEPHANIE: | But children are so used to visual input – on TV, video games, and so on. There are plenty of kids who wouldn't even <u>try</u> to read a book, so I think <u>comics can serve a really useful purpose</u>. |
| TREVOR: | You mean, it's better to read a comic than not to read at all? <u>Yes, I suppose you're right</u>. I just think it's sad when children don't read books. |
| STEPHANIE: | What about books for girls and books for boys? Does the course go into that? |
| TREVOR: | Yes, there's a module on it. For years, lots of stories, in English, at least, assumed that boys went out and did adventurous things and girls stayed at home and played with dolls. I was amazed <u>how many books were targeted at just one sex or the other</u>. Of course this reflects society as it is when the books are written. |
| STEPHANIE: | That's true. So it sounds as though you think it's a good course. |
| TREVOR: | Definitely. |

*Q23*

*Q24*

*Q25*

---

| | |
|---|---|
| TREVOR: | Have you been reading lots of children's stories, to help you decide whether to take the course? |
| STEPHANIE: | Yeah. I've gone as far back as the late seventeenth century, though I know there were earlier children's stories. |
| TREVOR: | So does that mean you've read Perrault's fairy tales? *Cinderella, The Sleeping Beauty*, and so on. |
| STEPHANIE: | Yes. They must be important, <u>because no stories of that type had been written before, these were the first</u>. Then there's *The Swiss Family Robinson*. |
| TREVOR: | I haven't read that. |
| STEPHANIE: | The English name makes it sound as though Robinson is the family's surname, but a more accurate translation would be *The Swiss Robinsons*, because it's about <u>a Swiss family who are shipwrecked, like Robinson Crusoe in the novel of a century earlier</u>. |
| TREVOR: | Well I never knew that! |
| STEPHANIE: | Have you read Hoffmann's *The Nutcracker and the Mouse King*? |
| TREVOR: | Wasn't that <u>the basis for Tchaikovsky's ballet *The Nutcracker*</u>? |
| STEPHANIE: | That's right. It has some quite bizarre elements. |
| TREVOR: | I hope you've read Oscar Wilde's *The Happy Prince*. It's probably my favourite children's story of all time. |
| STEPHANIE: | Mine too! And it's so surprising, because Wilde is best known for his plays, and most of them are very witty, but *The Happy Prince* is really moving. <u>I struggled with Tolkien's *The Lord of the Rings* – three long books, and I gave up after one</u>. |
| TREVOR: | It's extremely popular, though. |
| STEPHANIE: | Yeah, [as audio] but whereas something like *The Happy Prince* just carried me along with it, *The Lord of the Rings* took more effort than I was prepared to give it. |
| TREVOR: | I didn't find that – I love it. |
| STEPHANIE: | Another one I've read is *War Horse*. |
| TREVOR: | Oh yes. It's about the First World War, isn't it? <u>Hardly what you'd expect for a children's story</u>. |
| STEPHANIE: | Exactly, but it's been very successful. Have you read any ... |

*Q26*

*Q27*

*Q28*

*Q29*

*Q30*

# SECTION 4

In today's class I'm going to talk about marine archaeology, the branch of archaeology focusing on human interaction with the sea, lakes and rivers. It's the study of ships, cargoes, shipping facilities, and other physical remains. I'll give you an example, then go on to show how this type of research is being transformed by the use of the latest technology.

Atlit-Yam was a village on the coast of the eastern Mediterranean, which seems to have been thriving until around 7,000 BC. The residents kept cattle, caught fish and stored grain. They had wells for fresh water, many of their houses were built around a courtyard and were constructed of stone. The village contained an impressive monument: seven half-tonne stones standing in a semicircle around a <u>spring</u>, that might have been used for ceremonial purposes.   *Q31*

Atlit-Yam may have been destroyed swiftly by a tsunami, or climate change may have caused glaciers to melt and sea levels to rise, flooding the village gradually. Whatever the cause, it now lies ten metres below the surface of the Mediterranean, buried under sand at the bottom of the sea. It's been described as the largest and best preserved prehistoric settlement ever found on the seabed.

For marine archaeologists, Atlit-Yam is a treasure trove. Research on the buildings, <u>tools</u> and   *Q32* the human remains has revealed how the bustling village once functioned, and even what diseases some of its residents suffered from. But of course this is only one small village, one window into a lost world. For a fuller picture, researchers need more sunken settlements, but the hard part is finding them.

Underwater research used to require divers to find shipwrecks or artefacts, but in the second half of the twentieth century, various types of underwater vehicles were developed, some controlled from a ship on the surface, and some of them autonomous, which means they don't need to be operated by a person.

Autonomous underwater vehicles, or AUVs, are used in the oil industry, for instance, to create <u>maps</u> of the seabed before rigs and pipelines are installed. To navigate they use sensors,   *Q33* such as compasses and sonar. Until relatively recently they were very expensive, and so <u>heavy</u> that they had to be launched from a large vessel with a winch.   *Q34*

---

But the latest AUVs are much easier to manoeuvre – they can be launched from the shore or a small ship. And they're much cheaper, which makes them more accessible to research teams. They're also very sophisticated. They can communicate with each other and, for example, work out the most efficient way to survey a site, or to find particular objects on the seabed.

Field tests show the approach can work. For example, in a trial in 2015, three AUVs searched for wrecks at Marzamemi, off the coast of Sicily. The site is the final resting place of an ancient Roman ship, which sank in the sixth century AD while ferrying prefabricated <u>marble</u>   *Q35* elements for the construction of an early church. The AUVs mapped the area in detail, finding other ships carrying columns of the same material.

Creating an internet in the sea for AUVs to communicate is no easy matter. Wifi networks on land use electromagnetic waves, but in water these will only travel a few centimetres. Instead, a more complex mix of technologies is required. For short distances, AUVs can share data using <u>light</u>,   *Q36* while acoustic waves are used to communicate over long distances. But more creative solutions are also being developed, where an AUV working on the seabed offloads data to a second AUV, which then surfaces and beams the data home to the research team using a satellite.

There's also a system that enables AUVs to share information from seabed scans, and other data. So if an AUV surveying the seabed finds an intriguing object, it can share the coordinates of the object – that is, its position – with a nearby AUV that carries superior <u>cameras</u>, and arrange for that AUV to make a closer inspection of the object.     *Q37*

Marine archaeologists are excited about the huge potential of these AUVs for their discipline. One site where they're going to be deployed is the Gulf of Baratti, off the Italian coast. In 1974, a 2,000-year-old Roman vessel was discovered here, in 18 metres of water. When it sank, it was carrying <u>medical</u> goods, in wooden or tin receptacles. Its cargo gives us insight     *Q38* into the treatments available all those years ago, including tablets that are thought to have been dissolved to form a cleansing liquid for the <u>eyes</u>.     *Q39*

Other Roman ships went down nearby, taking their cargoes with them. Some held huge pots made of terracotta. Some were used for transporting cargoes of olive oil, and others held <u>wine</u>. In many cases it's only these containers that remain, while the wooden ships have been     *Q40* buried under silt on the seabed.

Another project that's about to ...

# Listening and Reading answer keys

## LISTENING

### Section 1, Questions 1–10

| | |
|---|---|
| 1 | Canadian |
| 2 | furniture |
| 3 | Park |
| 4 | 250 (sterling) |
| 5 | phone |
| 6 | 10(th) September |
| 7 | museum |
| 8 | time |
| 9 | blond(e) |
| 10 | 87954 82361 |

### Section 2, Questions 11–20

| | |
|---|---|
| 11&12 | *IN EITHER ORDER* |
| | A |
| | C |
| 13&14 | *IN EITHER ORDER* |
| | B |
| | E |
| 15 | B |
| 16 | B |
| 17 | C |
| 18 | A |
| 19 | A |
| 20 | C |

### Section 3, Questions 21–30

| | |
|---|---|
| 21 | B |
| 22 | A |
| 23 | C |
| 24 | B |
| 25 | A |
| 26 | B |
| 27 | A |
| 28 | F |
| 29 | G |
| 30 | C |

### Section 4, Questions 31–40

| | |
|---|---|
| 31 | industry |
| 32 | constant |
| 33 | direction |
| 34 | floor |
| 35 | predictable |
| 36 | bay |
| 37 | gates |
| 38 | fuel |
| 39 | jobs |
| 40 | migration |

## If you score …

| 0–18 | 19–27 | 28–40 |
|---|---|---|
| you are unlikely to get an acceptable score under examination conditions and we recommend that you spend a lot of time improving your English before you take IELTS. | you may get an acceptable score under examination conditions but we recommend that you think about having more practice or lessons before you take IELTS. | you are likely to get an acceptable score under examination conditions but remember that different institutions will find different scores acceptable. |

## TEST 1

# READING

### *Reading Section 1, Questions 1–14*

1 TRUE
2 FALSE
3 FALSE
4 NOT GIVEN
5 TRUE
6 FALSE
7 C
8 E
9 A
10 B
11 E
12 D
13 D
14 B

### *Reading Section 2, Questions 15–27*

15 Hospitality Department
16 academic calendar
17 1(st) October
18 nominated contractor
19 permits
20 Concorde Building
21 26 weeks
22 six weeks
23 £112.75
24 39 weeks
25 antenatal clinics
26 personal circumstances
27 grants

### *Reading Section 3, Questions 28–40*

28 ii
29 viii
30 vii
31 iii
32 vi
33 A
34 B
35 D
36 C
37 B
38 insects
39 tomb
40 eruption

## If you score …

| 0–23 | 24–31 | 32–40 |
|---|---|---|
| you are unlikely to get an acceptable score under examination conditions and we recommend that you spend a lot of time improving your English before you take IELTS. | you may get an acceptable score under examination conditions but we recommend that you think about having more practice or lessons before you take IELTS. | you are likely to get an acceptable score under examination conditions but remember that different institutions will find different scores acceptable. |

## TEST 2

# LISTENING

### Section 1, Questions 1–10

| | |
|---|---|
| 1 | 219 442 9785 |
| 2 | 10(th) October |
| 3 | manager |
| 4 | Cawley |
| 5 | knee |
| 6 | 3 weeks |
| 7 | tennis |
| 8 | running |
| 9 | shoulder |
| 10 | vitamins |

### Section 3, Questions 21–30

| | |
|---|---|
| 21 | B |
| 22 | C |
| 23 | A |
| 24 | A |
| 25 | E |
| 26 | D |
| 27 | A |
| 28 | H |
| 29 | G |
| 30 | C |

### Section 2, Questions 11–20

| | |
|---|---|
| 11 | B |
| 12 | C |
| 13 | C |
| 14 | B |
| 15 | A |
| 16 | H |
| 17 | D |
| 18 | F |
| 19 | A |
| 20 | E |

### Section 4, Questions 31–40

| | |
|---|---|
| 31 | dances |
| 32 | survival |
| 33 | clouds |
| 34 | festivals |
| 35 | comets |
| 36 | sky |
| 37 | instruments |
| 38 | thermometer |
| 39 | storms |
| 40 | telegraph |

## If you score...

| 0–17 | 18–26 | 27–40 |
|---|---|---|
| you are unlikely to get an acceptable score under examination conditions and we recommend that you spend a lot of time improving your English before you take IELTS. | you may get an acceptable score under examination conditions but we recommend that you think about having more practice or lessons before you take IELTS. | you are likely to get an acceptable score under examination conditions but remember that different institutions will find different scores acceptable. |

**TEST 2**

# READING

## *Reading Section 1,*
## *Questions 1–14*

1  C
2  A
3  B
4  E
5  D
6  A
7  B
8  FALSE
9  FALSE
10  NOT GIVEN
11  NOT GIVEN
12  TRUE
13  TRUE
14  TRUE

## *Reading Section 2,*
## *Questions 15–27*

15  clarification
16  discount
17  disciplinary
18  pain
19  storage
20  machinery
21  list
22  tool
23  energy
24  electronics
25  needs
26  permission
27  limitations

## *Reading Section 3,*
## *Questions 28–40*

28  E
29  C
30  B
31  A
32  D
33  B
34  G
35  A
36  permit
37  earthquake
38  storm
39  roadway
40  pedestrians

## If you score …

| 0–27 | 28–33 | 34–40 |
|---|---|---|
| you are unlikely to get an acceptable score under examination conditions and we recommend that you spend a lot of time improving your English before you take IELTS. | you may get an acceptable score under examination conditions but we recommend that you think about having more practice or lessons before you take IELTS. | you are likely to get an acceptable score under examination conditions but remember that different institutions will find different scores acceptable. |

## TEST 3

# LISTENING

### Section 1, Questions 1–10

| | |
|---|---|
| 1 | Tesla |
| 2 | microphone |
| 3 | exhibition |
| 4 | wifi |
| 5 | 45 |
| 6 | 135 |
| 7 | pool |
| 8 | airport |
| 9 | sea |
| 10 | clubs |

### Section 2, Questions 11–20

| | |
|---|---|
| **11&12** | **IN EITHER ORDER** |
| | A |
| | E |
| **13&14** | **IN EITHER ORDER** |
| | B |
| | E |
| 15 | F |
| 16 | A |
| 17 | E |
| 18 | G |
| 19 | D |
| 20 | C |

### Section 3, Questions 21–30

| | |
|---|---|
| 21 | 50 |
| 22 | regional |
| 23 | carnival |
| 24 | drummer |
| 25 | film |
| 26 | parade |
| 27 | D |
| 28 | B |
| 29 | E |
| 30 | F |

### Section 4, Questions 31–40

| | |
|---|---|
| 31 | violin |
| 32 | energy |
| 33 | complex |
| 34 | opera |
| 35 | disturbing |
| 36 | clarinet |
| 37 | diversity |
| 38 | physics |
| 39 | dance |
| 40 | Olympics |

## If you score...

| 0–17 | 18–27 | 28–40 |
|---|---|---|
| you are unlikely to get an acceptable score under examination conditions and we recommend that you spend a lot of time improving your English before you take IELTS. | you may get an acceptable score under examination conditions but we recommend that you think about having more practice or lessons before you take IELTS. | you are likely to get an acceptable score under examination conditions but remember that different institutions will find different scores acceptable. |

## TEST 3

# READING

### Reading Section 1, Questions 1–14

| | |
|---|---|
| 1 | B |
| 2 | E |
| 3 | D |
| 4 | C |
| 5 | C |
| 6 | B |
| 7 | A |
| 8 | FALSE |
| 9 | TRUE |
| 10 | FALSE |
| 11 | FALSE |
| 12 | TRUE |
| 13 | NOT GIVEN |
| 14 | FALSE |

### Reading Section 2, Questions 15–27

| | |
|---|---|
| 15 | emails |
| 16 | impact assessment |
| 17 | equipment |
| 18 | quality |
| 19 | crime |
| 20 | (computer) viruses |
| 21 | (confidential) helplines |
| 22 | questionnaire |
| 23 | account |
| 24 | 10 days |
| 25 | complete |
| 26 | employer |
| 27 | refund |

### Reading Section 3, Questions 28–40

| | |
|---|---|
| 28 | B |
| 29 | A |
| 30 | C |
| 31 | D |
| 32 | A |
| 33 | B |
| 34 | D |
| 35 | A |
| 36 | B |
| 37 | tsetse fly |
| 38 | immune system |
| 39 | proteins |
| 40 | cattle |

## If you score …

| 0–23 | 24–32 | 33–40 |
|---|---|---|
| you are unlikely to get an acceptable score under examination conditions and we recommend that you spend a lot of time improving your English before you take IELTS. | you may get an acceptable score under examination conditions but we recommend that you think about having more practice or lessons before you take IELTS. | you are likely to get an acceptable score under examination conditions but remember that different institutions will find different scores acceptable. |

## TEST 4

# LISTENING

### Section 1, Questions 1–10

| | |
|---|---|
| **1** | 85 |
| **2** | roses |
| **3** | trees |
| **4** | stage |
| **5** | speech |
| **6** | support |
| **7** | cabins |
| **8** | C |
| **9** | A |
| **10** | B |

### Section 2, Questions 11–20

| | |
|---|---|
| **11** | G |
| **12** | D |
| **13** | A |
| **14** | E |
| **15** | F |
| **16** | B |
| **17&18** | **IN EITHER ORDER** |
| | B |
| | D |
| **19&20** | **IN EITHER ORDER** |
| | A |
| | D |

### Section 3, Questions 21–30

| | |
|---|---|
| **21** | A |
| **22** | C |
| **23** | A |
| **24** | B |
| **25** | B |
| **26** | F |
| **27** | E |
| **28** | C |
| **29** | B |
| **30** | G |

### Section 4, Questions 31–40

| | |
|---|---|
| **31** | spring |
| **32** | tools |
| **33** | maps |
| **34** | heavy |
| **35** | marble |
| **36** | light |
| **37** | camera(s) |
| **38** | medical |
| **39** | eyes |
| **40** | wine |

## If you score...

| 0–18 | 19–27 | 28–40 |
|---|---|---|
| you are unlikely to get an acceptable score under examination conditions and we recommend that you spend a lot of time improving your English before you take IELTS. | you may get an acceptable score under examination conditions but we recommend that you think about having more practice or lessons before you take IELTS. | you are likely to get an acceptable score under examination conditions but remember that different institutions will find different scores acceptable. |

## TEST 4

# READING

### *Reading Section 1, Questions 1–14*

| | |
|---|---|
| 1 | D |
| 2 | B |
| 3 | C |
| 4 | F |
| 5 | D |
| 6 | G |
| 7 | E |
| 8 | B |
| 9 | TRUE |
| 10 | FALSE |
| 11 | FALSE |
| 12 | NOT GIVEN |
| 13 | TRUE |
| 14 | TRUE |

### *Reading Section 2, Questions 15–27*

| | |
|---|---|
| 15 | stadium |
| 16 | team |
| 17 | hygiene |
| 18 | storage |
| 19 | guaranteed |
| 20 | status |
| 21 | debts |
| 22 | profits |
| 23 | trading |
| 24 | internet |
| 25 | invoices |
| 26 | agent |
| 27 | penalty |

### *Reading Section 3, Questions 28–40*

| | |
|---|---|
| 28 | C |
| 29 | D |
| 30 | A |
| 31 | A |
| 32 | B |
| 33 | TRUE |
| 34 | NOT GIVEN |
| 35 | FALSE |
| 36 | TRUE |
| 37 | TRUE |
| 38 | FALSE |
| 39 | NOT GIVEN |
| 40 | NOT GIVEN |

## If you score …

| 0–24 | 25–32 | 33–40 |
|---|---|---|
| you are unlikely to get an acceptable score under examination conditions and we recommend that you spend a lot of time improving your English before you take IELTS. | you may get an acceptable score under examination conditions but we recommend that you think about having more practice or lessons before you take IELTS. | you are likely to get an acceptable score under examination conditions but remember that different institutions will find different scores acceptable. |

# Sample answers for Writing tasks

## TEST 1, WRITING TASK 1

### SAMPLE ANSWER

This is an answer written by a candidate who achieved a **Band 7.0** score.

Dear Mr and Mrs Collins,

My name is Carola. I have seen your advertisement in a magazine and I'm writing to you because I would like to be considered for the position you are offering. I really would like to work for you because I think it will be a good experience for you and me. I like to travel, know about different cultures and meet new people. I have never been to Australia but I'm pretty sure there a lot of thing to see and try. I have previous experience looking after children. Currently I'm working for an Irish family and I take care of for children whose ages vary from three to eight. I have to say that I've never thought that looking after children would be that rewarding. I enjoy spending time with them and I have learnt a lot. I'm really patient, tidy, reliable, and hard working.

In addition, I have just completed an first aids course.

If I had the chance to live with you would be great. I would spend my free time learning English, visiting turist attractions, trying local food and making new friends.

Thank you for taking the time to read my letter. Please feel free to contact me if you need further details and recomendations.

Kind regards,

Carola

Here is the examiner's comment:

> This answer presents a clear purpose with a consistent, appropriate tone. Each bullet point is clearly highlighted and covered, although there is room for some extension. Information and ideas are logically organised and cohesive devices are used appropriately. The range of vocabulary is sufficient to show some flexibility and precision, as well as use of collocation [*the position you are offering* | *previous experience* | *rewarding* | *taking the time to read my letter* | *contact me* | *further details*]. There are only occasional spelling errors [*first aids* | *turist* | *recomendations*]. There is a range of complex grammatical structures with frequent error-free sentences.

# TEST 1, WRITING TASK 2

## SAMPLE ANSWER

This is an answer written by a candidate who achieved a **Band 6.5** score.

Nowadays millions of online shops are doing business and develope rapidly. The majority of traditional shops concern if they will bankrupt soon due to the fast growing online shopping. However some people argue that a great deal of shops can still survive.

Firstly, the online shops always offer a very competitive price in order to obtain more and more consumers. They can always provide attractive promotion and sell the products in bottom price because they do not have to pay the extra rental for the physical shops. For example, in my own country, the daily turn over of Tao Bao on line shop is about 10 million, which is an astonishing amount.

Secondly, the people are keen on shopping on internet because it can save time. Especially the young generation are likely to browse the website of the shops at home in a comfortable atmosphere. They may flexibly select the goods that they like without the persuading from the shop staff. They can also compare the prices between various shops due to price – checking system.

However, some people said the traditional shops would still have their opportunities to retain their business. They suggest the owners of the chain stores or department stores can build up the online shops as well so as to maintain a stable business. Actually, there a lot of shops that have built up their online shops, such as the renowned sport shop Nike. All the shops should look for a correct manner to increase their business.

All in all, it is difficult to say that what is the advantage or disadvantage for online shopping. In my opinion, the owners of business should attain to check the trend of the business and quote a best price for keeping the purchasers.

Here is the examiner's comment:

> The candidate has covered all parts of the task but his/her position is not sufficiently clear for a higher band to be awarded. The response focuses on the advantages and disadvantages of online shopping, rather than on whether or not the writer agrees that this type of shopping will result in all shops in towns and cities closing. Organisation is logical, with appropriate use of cohesive devices and paragraphs and the range of vocabulary shows some less common items and use of collocation [*fast growing | competitive | keen on | browse the website | price-checking system | retain their business | renowned*]. There is a mix of simple and complex sentence forms and the meaning is clear, in spite of some errors.

# TEST 2, WRITING TASK 1

## MODEL ANSWER

This model has been prepared by an examiner as an example of a very good answer. However, please note that this is just one example out of many possible approaches.

Dear Sir or Madam

The latest edition of your travel magazine included an article about Cambridge, but this contained incorrect information. The writer described the University of Cambridge as being the oldest in the world whereas in fact the oldest university in the English-speaking world is in Oxford. The University of Cambridge was founded in 1209, but Oxford was known to have existed in 1096.

A magazine such as yours has an international reputation and is extremely influential with travel companies and individuals alike. It is essential that any information published should be accurate and reliable and I was genuinely surprised that the facts had not been checked prior to publication.

I feel that the least the magazine can do is to publish a correction and an apology in next month's magazine. I would also urge you to ensure that all factual information is thoroughly checked before publication.

Yours faithfully,

Alan Watson

## TEST 2, WRITING TASK 2

### SAMPLE ANSWER

This is an answer written by a candidate who achieved a **Band 8.0** score.

Some of the people believe that friends with exactly the same opinions on different topics are better than the ones that can argue with them.

On the one hand, having similar interests on hobbies is a reason to start a friendship. In this case people always have something to discuss. If your friend has the same view of particular problem as you do, he can help you to find a solution faster. Such friend will always support you and take your side in any argument. He will be there for you in any situation.

On the other hand, having equal opinions with you friend is sometimes boring. You always agree on every issue with each other and have no discussion or argument. If your friend disagrees with you, you can discuss both views, reach a compromise and come up with a suitable solution. But strong disagreement can often lead to a heated argument or even ruin your friendship.

In my opinion, friends should not agree on everything they are talking about. I think that this kind of friendship is boring and it is not likely to last for long. However, a friend with the same opinion as yours will definitely support your point of view in any discussion. And it is a wonderful thing, too.

In conclusion I would like to say that it is good to have different views on some topics or problems but you should be loyal to the opinion of your friend. Everyone should appreciate their friendship and shouldn't let stupid arguments ruin it.

Here is the examiner's comment:

> The candidate has discussed both sides of the topic and provided his/her own opinion in the final two paragraphs. Ideas for each point of view are developed and supported, but there is room for further extension. The writing shows logical organisation and sequencing of ideas, with good use of cohesive devices [*the ones that | In this case | On the one hand … On the other hand | this kind of friendship | the same opinion as yours*]. Paragraphing is used sufficiently and appropriately. The range of vocabulary includes some less common items and collocations [*support you | take your side in | be there for you | reach a compromise | come up with*] and there are only rare errors [*you / your friend*]. There is a wide range of complex structures with very few errors (there are two cases of missing articles), but both vocabulary and grammatical range lack the sophistication expected from a Band 9 answer.

# TEST 3, WRITING TASK 1

## SAMPLE ANSWER

This is an answer written by a candidate who achieved a **Band 7.0** score.

Dear Sir or Madam,

I am writing to you to provide a feedback on the "Kitchen Wonders" cookery course I have taken recently. As my cooking had become more and more complimented since, I would like to take this opportunity to express my appreciation for the evolution I have attained from the course.

Albeit a short and basic course, it contained useful tips on using cutlery and cookware which were entirely new to me. Having always cooked by instinct these tips ~~(enabled)~~ brought to light simple mistakes I had been making, which now I avoid. Moreover, I particularly enjoyed the "Kitchen Hacks" module, and its techniques have brought my cooking skills to a new level.

I have been using these lessons on weekends, when I normally cook for my family, and the difference is clear. The effect the course had on my dishes has been remarked on some occasions, and this new found ability has been raising expectations as the word spreads throughout my relatives. Still, I am confident they shall not be disappointed.

I intend on honing this skill further, especially since the course did not address dessert-making. Should such a course be offered, I would be delighted to enroll and keep collecting awestruck expressions from my relatives. I really appreciate the results your course has provided me, and I look forward to even more.

Sincerely,

Paulo

Here is the examiner's comment:

> The response covers all the bullet points and develops them at some length. The purpose is clear and the only inconsistency in tone is the use of [*Sincerely*] to close the letter. Information and ideas are logically organised and there is a clear progression throughout. There is a range of cohesive devices, used appropriately [*Albeit | it | which | these tips | Moreover*], for example. The range of vocabulary is wide enough to show some less common items and collocations [*cooked by instinct | brought to light | Kitchen Hacks | new found ability | honing my skills | awestruck*], with only minor errors [*The effect the course had on my dishes has been remarked* (upon) *on some occasions | enroll / enrol*]. There is a variety of complex structures, with frequent error-free sentences and good control of punctuation with only a few errors.

# TEST 3, WRITING TASK 2

## SAMPLE ANSWER

This is an answer written by a candidate who achieved a **Band 6.5** score.

In the world, there are things we can buy paying money But, at the same time there are things that we'll never be able to get thought we are milianair.

We can make ourselves spending money to buy visible items, such as expensive cars, bags, houses, clothes and so on. A friend of mine, when she is stressful she like to go shopping to get rid of the stress. Luckily she is rich so she is satisfied and happy after purchasing as many things as possible. Also, money can be very important for some things which are not visible. For example, if any of family members is illed requring a expensive surgery money becomes the most important factor to decide to proceed with the surgery or just suffer without having the surgery.

We can not only make ourselves happy when we have lots of money, we can also be happy with some things that we never buy with money.
My parents were not rich when I was a child. I desired to get toys and pretty clethings but the couldn't afford to buy them. I was disappointed that I could not have those things while my friends were having.
But my parents brought me up with unlimited love and they became my best friend to listen to me when I was in truble and needed adviie. As a result my childhood was happy and I grew up having positive way of thinking instead of complainng for the things my parents couldn't buy for me.

In conclusion through my experience, we can make our lives convenient when having enough money. But, we do not need to be frustrated or desperate with not having lots of money.
Happiness depends on our mind set and it is always subjective to change if the amount of money is considered a lot or little.
By focusing on what we have on our hands now and drive to achieve what we want to gain, we can always be happy.

Here is the examiner's comment:

> The candidate has addressed all parts of the task and presents a well-developed response. Ideas are relevant, extended and supported throughout. The candidate's task response is the best aspect of this piece of writing. Ideas are logically organised, with some use of cohesive devices, and there is a clear overall progression, but paragraphing is inconsistent and not always logical. The range of vocabulary is adventurous [*proceed with the surgery* | *unlimited love* | *positive way of thinking* | *frustrated* | *desperate*], but there also errors in some quite basic items [*thought* / though | *milianair* / millionaire | *stressful* / stressed | *illed* / ill | *clethings* / clothes | *the* / they |*truble* / trouble | *adviie* / advice | *complainng* / complaining], which limits the rating on Lexical Resource. There is a mix of simple and complex sentence forms, with a fair degree of accuracy, but a wider range and better control over punctuation would perhaps result in a higher score here.

# TEST 4, WRITING TASK 1

## SAMPLE ANSWER

This is an answer written by a candidate who achieved a **Band 6.0** score.

Dear Mr. Tremain,

I saw your concert recently at Manchester Hall and I thought your performance was very touching and excellent. I felt deeply connected with the lyrics in your songs. I am a current music student at Oxford university and our school is having a musical performance next week. The play relates well to your latest song and I would be very greatful if you can help with me musical activities by providing a more detail insight to your lyric. Also, could you give us some tips about performing as this is our first performance. By giving an insight to your lyric, our drama and musical team a deeper connection to the song, which is what we really need. I hope I am not asking for too much. My team really looks up to you and it would mean the world if you write back.

Thank You for reading this letter and I hope to hear from you soon.

Yours Sincerly,

Here is the examiner's comment:

> The candidate covers all three bullet points, but there is room for development of the ideas presented. There is an overall progression in the response, but it could be improved by using separate paragraphs for each topic. The range of vocabulary is sufficient for the task, with some attempts at less common items [*lyrics* | *insight*] and with only a few mistakes in spelling and word form [*greatful* / grateful | *detail* / detailed], though more specific vocabulary would improve the writing [*the play* / performance?]. Both simple and complex sentence structures are used, with some accuracy, but there appears to be a missing section [*our drama and musical team* (would obtain?) *a deeper connection to the song*].

# TEST 4, WRITING TASK 2

## MODEL ANSWER

This model has been prepared by an examiner as an example of a very good answer. However, please note that this is just one example out of many possible approaches.

Nowadays many people work long hours, leaving them little time for leisure activities. There are some advantages in this situation, but personally I feel there are more disadvantages. The advantages include the possibility of earning more money, if the employer pays overtime for extra hours worked. This can be a real bonus if someone is saving with a particular goal in mind: a holiday, for example, or saving to buy a house or flat. Another advantage might be that more time spent at work enables a more thorough knowledge and understanding of the job. Some professions such as law and accountancy require familiarity with a wide range of rules and requirements and these cannot all be learned through study; they have to be learned on the job. For younger people there is also the sheer stimulus of being involved in something they enjoy, so that they do not object to, or count, the hours they spend at work.

Unfortunately, if people do not have enough time to relax, there are quite major risks associated with this. Health often suffers, either physically or mentally, and sometimes both. Taking time out for physical leisure activities has positive effects on health through the release of chemicals that make us feel better both physically and mentally. Other leisure activities may involve spending time with a group of people, activating skills other than those used at work and thus encouraging supportive social networks.

Friendships can also be weakened because of not making enough time to stay in touch, but using only a little of your free time to have a meal or go to the cinema with someone helps to maintain that friendship. Listening to your friend's problems, or talking through your own, reinforces your relationship with them, as well as allowing you to switch off mentally from the things that have been happening at work. This 'distancing' from work helps you to get things back into perspective and can sometimes help you to find solutions to matters that have been bothering you.

Within a family situation a partner may feel neglected if the other one spends long hours away at work, or a child may feel neglected because mummy/daddy is never around for birthdays, school performances or a vital sports match. This lack of involvement is a major contributor to family breakdown, which in turn has wider repercussions in our society.

Work is a major part of our lives and it is to be hoped that many find it enjoyable, challenging and stimulating, but it is important to recognise the need for a work–life balance and to ensure that this is put into practice.

# Sample answer sheets

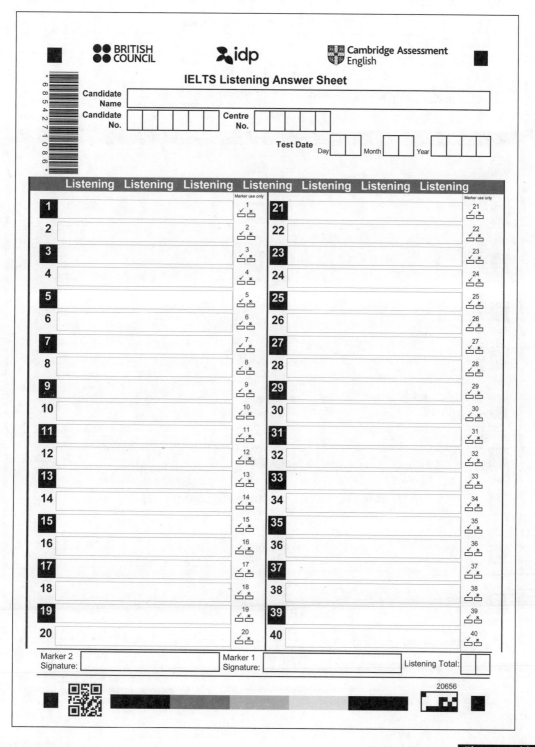

BRITISH COUNCIL

idp

Cambridge Assessment English

**IELTS Listening Answer Sheet**

Candidate Name

Candidate No.

Centre No.

Test Date   Day   Month   Year

Listening Listening Listening Listening Listening Listening Listening

Marker use only

| | |
|---|---|
| 1 | 21 |
| 2 | 22 |
| 3 | 23 |
| 4 | 24 |
| 5 | 25 |
| 6 | 26 |
| 7 | 27 |
| 8 | 28 |
| 9 | 29 |
| 10 | 30 |
| 11 | 31 |
| 12 | 32 |
| 13 | 33 |
| 14 | 34 |
| 15 | 35 |
| 16 | 36 |
| 17 | 37 |
| 18 | 38 |
| 19 | 39 |
| 20 | 40 |

Marker 2 Signature:

Marker 1 Signature:

Listening Total:

20656

*Sample answer sheets*

## IELTS Reading Answer Sheet

Candidate Name

Candidate No.

Centre No.

Test Module ☐ Academic ☐ General Training

Test Date  Day   Month   Year

**Reading   Reading   Reading   Reading   Reading   Reading   Reading**

Marker use only

| | |
|---|---|
| 1 | 21 |
| 2 | 22 |
| 3 | 23 |
| 4 | 24 |
| 5 | 25 |
| 6 | 26 |
| 7 | 27 |
| 8 | 28 |
| 9 | 29 |
| 10 | 30 |
| 11 | 31 |
| 12 | 32 |
| 13 | 33 |
| 14 | 34 |
| 15 | 35 |
| 16 | 36 |
| 17 | 37 |
| 18 | 38 |
| 19 | 39 |
| 20 | 40 |

Marker 2 Signature:

Marker 1 Signature:

Reading Total:

61788

**BRITISH COUNCIL**

**idp**

**Cambridge Assessment English**

## IELTS Writing Answer Sheet - TASK 1

Candidate Name

Candidate No.

Centre No.

Test Module ☐ Academic ☐ General Training

Test Date   Day   Month   Year

If you need more space to write your answer, use an additional sheet and write in the space provided to indicate how many sheets you are using:   Sheet   of

### Writing   Task 1   Writing   Task 1   Writing   Task 1   Writing   Task 1

Do not write below this line

Do not write in this area. Please continue your answer on the other side of this sheet.

23505

*Sample answer sheets*

**BRITISH COUNCIL**

**idp**

**Cambridge Assessment English**

**IELTS Writing Answer Sheet - TASK 2**

Candidate Name

Candidate No.

Centre No.

Test Module ☐ Academic ☐ General Training

Test Date Day Month Year

If you need more space to write your answer, use an additional sheet and write in the space provided to indicate how many sheets you are using: Sheet ☐ of ☐

Writing Task 2 Writing Task 2 Writing Task 2 Writing Task 2

Do not write below this line

Do not write in this area. Please continue your answer on the other side of this sheet.

39507

© UCLES 2019   Photocopiable

# Acknowledgements

The authors and publishers acknowledge the following sources of copyright material and are grateful for the permissions granted. While every effort has been made, it has not always been possible to identify the sources of all the material used, or to trace all copyright holders. If any omissions are brought to our notice, we will be happy to include the appropriate acknowledgements on reprinting and in the next update to the digital edition, as applicable.

**Reading – Test 1:** Text adapted from 'Transition care (care after a hospital stay)' by Myagedcare. Copyright © Commonwealth of Australia as represented by the Department of Health. Reproduced with kind permission; Text adapted from 'LTU Car Parking Policy AY 2018/19'. Copyright © 2018 Leeds Trinity University. Reproduced with kind permission; Text contains public sector information licensed under the Open Government Licence v3.0.; **Test 2:** Text extracted from WorkSmart, the work advice website of the Trades Union Congress *www.worksmart.org.uk*. Reproduced with kind permission; Text adapted from '8 Steps to Achieving Work-Life Balance' by Joanna Ireland. Copyright © TopResume, a Talent Inc. company, *www.topresume.com*. Reproduced with kind permission; Text adapted from 'Golden Gate Bridge' by History.com Editors. Courtesy of A+E Networks. Reproduced with permission; **Test 3:** Text adapted from 'Monitoring at work'. Copyright © Citizens Advice. Reproduced with kind permission; **Test 4:** *The Independent* for the adapted text from '10 best travel wallets' by Becca Meier. Copyright © 2017, *The Independent*. Reproduced with permission; Text adapted from 'How do I claim back money for my delayed train?' by Harry Rose. Copyright © 2017, *Which?*. Reproduced with kind permission; Text adapted from 'The many faces of the Swiss postbus' by Vitali Vitaliev. Copyright © 2017 Syon Geographical Ltd. Reproduced with permission.

# Authentic examination papers: what do we mean?

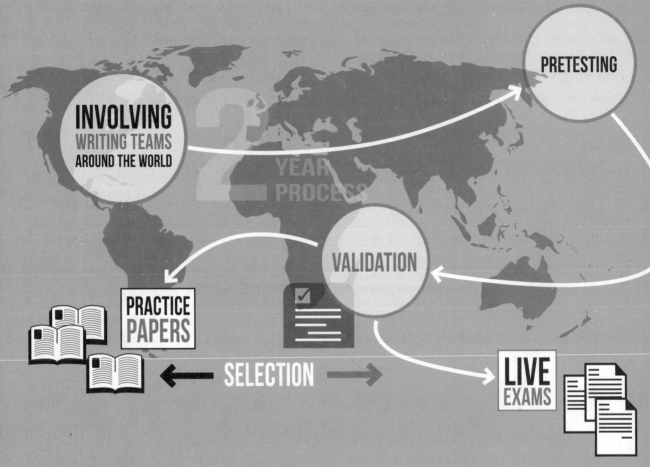

INVOLVING
WRITING TEAMS
AROUND THE WORLD

2 YEAR PROCESS

PRETESTING

VALIDATION

PRACTICE
PAPERS

← SELECTION →

LIVE
EXAMS

## Practice makes perfect!

### Get more out of authentic practice tests

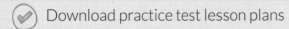 Download practice test lesson plans

Get tips and tricks to use in your classroom

**practicemakesperfect.cambridge.org**

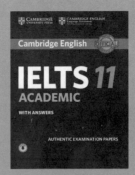

LSC @ Legalaid · ab · Ca ·
Subj: - Name, Date of Birth

Payee: -
Act #:
LSC - 000243749.

1850